PENGUIN BOOKS
Philosophy of the Home

Emanuele Coccia is a philosopher teaching at the École des Hautes Études en Sciences Sociales in Paris. He has lectured and taught courses at several universities, including Tokyo, Buenos Aires, Amsterdam, Harvard and Columbia, and collaborated on many art exhibitions in France and Italy. He is the author of numerous books translated into several languages, including *The Life of Plants* (2018). He is a columnist for *Libération* and collaborates with *Le Monde* and *La Repubblica*. He is currently writing a book on the relationship between fashion and philosophy with Gucci's creative director Alessandro Michele

Richard Dixon lives and works in Italy. His translations include works by Giacomo Leopardi, Umberto Eco, Roberto Calasso, Paolo Volponi and Antonio Moresco. His translation of *The Experience of Pain* by Carlo Emilio Gadda is published by Penguin Classics.

T0267947

Philosophy of the Home

Domestic Space and Happiness

EMANUELE COCCIA

Translated from the Italian by
Richard Dixon

PENGUIN BOOKS

PENGUIN BOOKS

UK | USA | Canada | Ireland | Australia
India | New Zealand | South Africa

Penguin Books is part of the Penguin Random House group of companies
whose addresses can be found at global.penguinrandomhouse.com

Penguin
Random House
UK

First published in Italian as *Filosofia della casa. Lo spazio domestico e la felicità*, 2021
This translation first published by Penguin Books, 2024

002

Copyright © Giulio Einaudi editore s.p.a., Turin, 2021
Translation and notes copyright © Richard Dixon, 2024

The moral rights of the author and the translator have been asserted

Set in 11.75/15 pt Garamond MT Std
Typeset by Jouve (UK), Milton Keynes
Printed and bound in Great Britain by Clays Ltd, Elcograf S.p.A.

The authorized representative in the EEA is Penguin Random House Ireland,
Morrison Chambers, 32 Nassau Street, Dublin D02 YH68

A CIP catalogue record for this book is available from the British Library

ISBN: 978–1–802–06101–7

www.greenpenguin.co.uk

To my daughter

Contents

vii

CONTENTS

Introduction

Home beyond the City

Philosophy has always had a special relationship with the city. It was born there, it learned to talk there, and it was there – always within city walls – that it imagined its history and its future. Tales of its past speak of streets, marketplaces, public gatherings, places of worship and palaces of power. The story of philosophy resembles not so much a novel as a Grand Tour: this esoteric and elitist branch of knowledge evolved by migrating and being transmitted through the cities of different nations and continents.

In this imaginary cartographic biography, pride of place must be given to the city of Crotone, once in Magna Graecia, now in Calabria, southern Italy, where Pythagoras founded his School in 532 BC. There, it is said, philosophy found its name, which was originally a term of irony. The definition of 'philosophy' in the language of that era was something halfway between the expression of a desire to learn and a declaration of amateurishness by someone refusing to be considered an 'expert'. Not far from Crotone, on this ideal map, would be Athens, where Plato founded his Academy in 387 BC and Aristotle founded his Lyceum in 335 BC: it was there that philosophy received its definitive consecration and began to be identified with the city itself. If philosophy in Crotone was the rule governing the life of a community of individuals who had chosen to live apart from others, in Athens it sought to embody the relationships that unite all other human beings. But it was in Syracuse in Sicily, it seems, that philosophy yielded to the temptation to appropriate power, to assume sovereignty; and here it became a source of law that regulated actions and opinions, and a guardian of truth that the city could recognize and cultivate. In Rome this desire to become 'living justice' (*lex animata*) became so radical as to identify thought with law and legislation. The map should also include Paris, where philosophy became a subject to be taught, and Frankfurt, where it learned to be a challenging force that prevented all cities from becoming the same.

The list of cities in which philosophy became

established and where it is said to have thrived is endless. Contrary to what we might think, this imaginary geography is not just 'Western' or European. It is said, for example, that in Alexandria, in Egypt, philosophy encountered the spirit of Jewish culture and religion, and blended with it, above all in the writings of Philo, which would prove so important in the way that divinity is now discussed. It was at Hippo, a city which stood in present-day Annaba, in Algeria, that philosophy learned to speak in the first person – to say 'I' – and to embed itself deep in the body of daily human life: it was in this city that Augustine wrote his *Confessions*. Baghdad is where philosophy served as a cultural meeting point: here, from AD 832, the personal library of Caliph Harun al-Rashid was transformed into a 'house of wisdom', open for encounters between philosophers, astronomers and mathematicians, and for dialogue between different languages, cultures and religions.

This urban biography of philosophy includes not just metropolises and imperial capitals. Philosophy sometimes needed to dwell in provinces or on city outskirts. Many of the most powerful and touching parts of its history were written in very modest towns: Spinoza's *Ethics*, for example, was composed at Voorburg, on the edge of The Hague, as well as in the city itself; Hegel wrote *Phenomenology of the Spirit* in the small city of Jena, where such leading figures of German Romanticism as the Schlegel brothers, Novalis, Ludwig Tieck and Clemens Brentano lived. Each of these cities seems to have its mark indelibly tattooed on the body of philosophy, producing a single hieroglyphic of thought capable of transmitting and harmonizing the atmosphere, the light, the existence of each one.

And yet this long diorama is hiding something, or rather, trying to forget it. Athens or Rome, Baghdad or Alexandria are no more than mesmerizing and alluring backdrops, certainly greater and more solid than any other theatre, but they have the same substance as a vast shadow play. Every city on the planet, regardless of whether it has played a part in the birth of philosophy, is an immense, decorated open-air stage that allows us to imagine ourselves elsewhere, to lose sight of the place in which we really are. All of us pretend not to realize it, but none of us really live in a city. None of us can do so, for cities are, literally, uninhabitable. We can spend endless hours in them, we

INTRODUCTION

can experience supreme or hellish moments in
them. We can stop off at the office, wander the
shops, stroll through a maze of streets and alleys,
or closet ourselves in theatres or cinemas, sit outside bars, eat at restaurants, or go to sports grounds
or swimming pools. But sooner or later we must
return home, for we only ever live on this planet
thanks to – and inside – a place we call home. Its
form is quite irrelevant: it might be a hotel, an
apartment, a room just large enough for a single
bed, or a skyscraper. It might be a shabby cluttered
bedsit, poor as a garret, or as splendid as a royal
palace. It might be built of stone or made from
animal hides that fold up and can be carried about.
But beneath, within and behind the city there is
always a home in which we can live. A life that
attempts to fit into the urban landscape, to live
there with no mediation, is destined to die: the
only true and absolute citizens are the homeless,
the *clochards*. Theirs is a vulnerable life, one which,
by definition, runs the risk of death.

It is only ever through the mediation of a home
that we live in a city. I have only lived in cities –
whether Paris or Berlin, Tokyo or New York – in
which I have existed thanks to bedrooms and

5

kitchens; thanks to chairs, desks, wardrobes, bathtubs and radiators.

It's not just a problem of space. Living somewhere doesn't mean being surrounded by something, nor occupying a certain portion of land. It means embarking on a relationship with certain things – and with certain people – that is so intense that it makes happiness part and parcel of our breathing. A home creates an intensity that changes our way of being, and everything which forms part of its magic circle. Architecture or biology are of little importance. We don't build homes to protect ourselves from bad weather, or to pass them down to our children, or to satisfy our aesthetic taste. Every home is a purely moral reality: we build homes to give a form of intimacy to the portion of the world – comprising objects, people, animals, plants, atmospheres, events, images and memories – that makes happiness possible.

On the other hand, our very act of building homes is evidence that morality – or happiness – can never be reduced to a set of precepts governing our attitudes, or to a discipline of feelings, or of behaving considerately, or to a form of mental hygiene. It is a material order that involves objects and people, an economy that interweaves objects and affections – our own and those of others – into the minimal spatial unit of 'care' that exists in the home. Happiness is not an emotion, nor a purely subjective experience. It is the arbitrary and transitory harmony that brings together objects and people in a relationship of physical and spiritual intimacy.

And yet, philosophy has always had very little to say about the home. It has neglected the domestic space to which it is bound more intimately than to any city on the planet, as if intoxicated by the dream – associated for centuries with male identity – of excelling in society, of having power and influence in the city. And so, after the first great Greek treatises on *oikonomia* (the order and management of the home), whose influence was unequalled, philosophy dismissed the domestic space from the horizon of its concerns. This neglect was anything but innocent – it is why the home has become a space in which wrongs, constrictions, injustices and inequalities have been hidden, forgotten and unconsciously and mechanically reproduced over centuries. It is in the home and through the home, for example, that inequality between the sexes was generated, affirmed and justified. It is in the home and through the home, and in the arrangement of property that constitutes and embodies it, that society is organized in economic inequality. It is through the modern home – a space which, with a few exceptions, can accommodate humans alone – that the radical opposition between the human and the non-human, between the city and the forest, between the 'civilized' and the wild, has been built and consolidated.

For philosophy, neglecting the home has been a way of neglecting ourselves. This hidden sense of dignity has indeed also been the incubator for a large number of ideas that have nourished the planet throughout its history. It is in this space of variable geometry, which is never exactly the same even in the same city, that flesh becomes word.

Philosophy's neglect of the home has led to unhappiness, rendering happiness unthinkable and subordinating it to the city and to politics. By abandoning the home to forces of genealogy – to inheritance and ownership – philosophy has compelled it to limit its concerns to physical anatomy and to banish from its walls, into the city, all that has anything to do with true happiness. If happiness has become a shadow-play it is precisely because, removed from the domestic environment – which could no longer accommodate it – it has become a political matter, a purely urban reality. The modern city, on the other hand, is an extraordinary invention: a disparate set of places, techniques and systems built in opposition to domestic order, with the task of producing the freedom and happiness that it wasn't possible to generate at home. In the city, through labour, consumption, education, culture or simple entertainment, it is possible to overcome the strange state of naturalized negligence, or unexpected naturalness, in which things do not change according to the dictates of a supposed 'biological' order or prime necessity. For centuries, the world in which equality with others was possible, at least on paper, began as soon as people closed their front doors behind them. Outside the home – in schools, cinemas, theatres, restaurants, bars, museums, discotheques, shops, parks and streets, but also in parliaments, churches, synagogues and mosques – was where the world offered real experience. Outside the home was a place populated with faces, with objects, with ideas all too powerful and too great to remain inside the closed environment of bedrooms and kitchens.

From Plato to Hobbes, from Rousseau to Rawls, the modern city has been philosophy's great sleight of hand: a real philosophical *trompe l'œil*, an open-air dream of freedom and collective phantasmagoria whose primary task was to make sure the home was forgotten, to reduce it as far as possible to a storeroom in which something could be left and forgotten with no feelings of guilt.

In this, philosophy is not alone. The home has been the subject of theoretical neglect; it's as if, over time, it had been transformed through its own will into a strange kind of machine that has to gather everything we cannot talk about in public or need to forget. For centuries, the home was the 'leftovers': that which remained after the show had ended, all that we never managed to share with others.

Unlike cities, the homes that make up their corpus are places whose history we only occasionally share publicly: apart from very rare exceptions it is impossible to have a clear idea about who has lived in a particular place, how their homes were furnished over the decades or what events played out there. And even when such a memory exists, it is never shared in the same way as the memory of the city. The overwhelming majority of homes are still places that remain publicly anonymous, with no name that can last over time. They are identifiable only through topographical coordinates – through an address or a name plaque which can, by definition, always be changed. It's enough to compare the home with any city to realize how strange that is: what would we think about cities if, instead of calling them Venice, Marseilles, Beijing or Dakar, we used a longitude or latitude, or name plaques that changed every five or ten years?

It's as if every home demanded not to be acknowledged over time, insisting on the power to wipe out its own history so that it could start another without any memories being retained. As if a home were a self-cleaning vehicle that allowed life to leave no traces. As if the time inside it could not accumulate in the form of a history, but was akin to a continuously reawakened consciousness that recalled nothing that had taken place before it went to sleep and while it was dreaming.

Over the last few decades, however, something of this mechanism of marginalization and oblivion has been shattered. The abundance of objects designed, produced and consumed by industry has been directed towards populating domestic spaces above all else. The invention of television has caused the psychic barrier between life in the city and the internal life of the home to collapse, bringing the public domain into private living spaces. Social media has created a public domain that is portable and has no geographical anchor and is modelled almost entirely in the image and likeness of our apartments.

This intrusion of the city and its spectres has radically changed our way and rhythm of life, but it hasn't yet succeeded in radically modifying its structure. It's as if, by leaving our home in search of happiness, we have been left imprisoned in a dream of men and women about whom we know nothing. The bathrooms, kitchens, corridors and bedrooms in which we spend at least half our lives – and indeed the very division of the home into these categories – are the projection of thousands of anonymous, ancient 'egos'. The home today is a kind of Platonic cave, the moral ruin of an archaeological humanity. It is only by revolutionizing the way in which we give form and content to the experience of home that we will manage once again to make the world a place where a common, shared happiness is possible.

Modern philosophy has steered everything towards the city, but the future of the world can only be domestic. We need to think about the home. We urgently need to turn this planet into a proper place in which to live, or rather, we must each turn our home into a true planet, a space that can accommodate everyone and everything. The modern-day project of globalizing the city must be replaced by one that opens up our houses and apartments so that they are in touch with the Earth.

I

MOVING

They were everywhere and had transformed the sitting room into an ugly maze of cardboard, adhesive tape and anxiety. I have always hated packing cases: their colour dampens all enthusiasm. I was about to lift one of them when I was struck motionless by a confused jumble of memories – how many times had I repeated that same gesture? I paused for a moment and tried to count and remember the moves I'd already made: thirty.

I could get no further. It was July. I'd been in Paris for three years and had only two days to 'shut up shop'. Forty-eight hours to buy eighty packing cases, assemble them, seal my life – my clothing, crockery, books, photos, memories – inside them, then hire a van, load it up, unload it again, carry everything into my new apartment, and disinter my life in a place I barely knew. I was moving in with my then girlfriend. We were expecting a child. We had taken a sublease on an apartment in the south of the city. It belonged to a friend who had moved to Berkeley, California. We wanted to take our time looking for 'a home of our own'. We wanted to create a space in which everything – furniture, walls, objects, but also feelings and affections – resembled what we hoped we would be together. Moving home is the secular and everyday equivalent of what in mythology is the last judgement: the damned are separated from the elect, a clear and distinct dividing line is drawn between the present and what we hope will be the past; everything is done to make sure that this line corresponds to that between pain and happiness. These are rites of passage and of metamorphosis.

We stayed in that temporary apartment for four months, and then, just a few weeks before moving, we found a place at Montreuil, on the eastern out-skirts of Paris. It was an area where artists, designers and young couples from the capital went to live, with larger open spaces, greener parks, like those of a provincial village.

We lived there for less than a year. I was invited to the United States, and we went to New York. For nine months, we and our young child Colette settled on the Upper West Side, close to the university where I was working, in a small apartment in one of those typical New York buildings with the doorman who watches over the entrance night and day from behind an enormous desk. Colette took her first steps there. I had just a couple of bags when I arrived. When I left, I had dozens of packing cases and much of that year's life had to be shipped back separately.

Back in Europe, we returned to the same apartment on the outskirts of Paris, but once again we were only there for a short while. My girlfriend left me after a year. So, once again, I packed up my life and my anxieties in a few cardboard boxes, started looking for a home, and went to live elsewhere.

Nor was this my last move. It went on for years, averaging one move every twelve months, only rarely within the same city. Very often it was to different countries, thousands of miles apart. Moving then meant having to leave behind almost everything I had, not just furniture.

My most recent move was eighteen months ago, to an apartment a few yards from the church of Saint-Germain, at the top of a seventeenth-century building, one of those that seem to lean perilously inwards when seen from outside. Unlike the *hôtels particuliers* of the same period scattered around the city, this has no magnificence and is showing its age. The low-relief plaques that decorate one side of the inner courtyard, next to a wall overgrown with ivy, are worn and grey with rain and smog. In the courtyard there's a half-open stairway that leads to my apartment. The walls there have aged too. No one has ever dared touch them. The wrinkles can be seen, but here they are marks of beauty. I've never felt so much love for the place I've lived in.

All the same, I probably won't stay here long. And yet, apart from the impending anxiety of having to face packing cases (a hundred and fifty of which are hibernating in the cellar), I have no fear of another move.

I've opened and closed the doors of over thirty homes. Thinking about it now, I've never tried picturing them side by side. It would be like imagining a small neighbourhood of totally incompatible worlds. Each would contain faces that barely recognized each other and would find very little in common with the life I'm living now.

Thirty collections of walls that gathered, protected and cradled everything I considered mine – though not in terms of possession, not in a legal sense.

Much of that 'mine' was not linked to me by a bond of ownership I could have established in any court of law. It didn't relate just to things: above all, they were memories, feelings, experiences and, especially, the lives of others. These had never belonged to me, but they were also mine.

Thirty homes, more than anything, are thirty spaces of different shapes and sizes which have said 'I' on my behalf. None of these homes could find the right accent: I never managed to hear them as my own voice. Each was my home for a few months, or a few years, but in none of them did I come to think 'I am home'. It was as if I had been condemned to keep on moving while some people managed to get it right first time: to open a door, walk in and never leave. Yet it has been this very repetition that opened doors to the *idea* of home: it is this involuntary domestic promiscuity that has compelled me to examine everything that makes a place a home, which has enabled me, like Don Giovanni, to catalogue them. Almost none of these features has anything to do with architecture and design. A home is the epitome of moral reality: a mental and material artefact that makes us inhabit the world better than our nature would otherwise allow.

For this very reason a theory about the home marks the beginning and end of moral theory – that disparate composite of wisdoms and stories that allows us to understand how to live happily with others, here and now. A home is this: a first, never complete, attempt at creating an overlap between our own true happiness and the world. It is the place where every moral system admits that it cannot concern itself only with abstractions – with will and character, justice and happiness, action and virtue – but has to address the world in its humbler, material dimensions. A theory of happiness and justice must necessarily become a theory of the passionate transformation of the world, of things, of matter.

We are beings that, in order to be happy, need to manipulate and modify everything around us: it is not enough for us to know the world and not enough to respect the rules of good conduct. Science is not enough, and law is not enough. 'Home' is simply the name for this aggregate of techniques we use to mediate between ourselves and the planet, a cosmic curve that, for an instant, brings together mind and matter, essence and world.

It's through moving that I have understood this. It seems obvious, but it's the move that makes the home. And for one very simple reason: we have always initially been strangers to the homes we have later loved and inhabited. We have always entered our homes from outside. We are strangers also, and above all, to our own happiness: it is deceptive to imagine that happiness lies within. If it did, we wouldn't need to live, to experience, to encounter others and involve ourselves so inextricably in their lives, to eat, or graze our knees, or get too close to things that hurt us. There is nothing natural about our happiness. On the other hand, it's when we try to be happy that that work of self-manipulation and refinement we call 'culture' begins. We don't need to leave the home and go into the city – into the political sphere – for happiness to become something cultural and artificial. It is morality – in other words, happiness – that makes us cultural beings: beings committed to transforming ourselves and everything around us in order to reach a perfection greater than what we currently have. We are all strangers, yet we manage each time to make a home for ourselves. To build a form of happiness.

Moving is the first moment, the moment of choice. We imagine that homes exist before those who live in them, that they are waiting only to be occupied. And yet their walls and roofs, wardrobes, beds, tables and clothing only become a home after a strange and lengthy ceremony whose rules we all know, if only unconsciously. Every home is created, first, through an act of choice: a series of gestures through which we gather a relatively incompatible set of objects, people and walls, and transform them into a special place – into our world. It's almost never the place in which we spend most time, but it's where we go back each day: our place of return. This choice is arbitrary, for we have nothing 'naturally' in common with a given space, with a set of objects or with a group of living beings. Even with our parents, to be at home with them always requires enormous mental and physical effort, and endless strategies.

Indeed, choice alone is not enough: homemaking requires a still longer process of habituation, of transformation from the stranger we were into a native, and that even more tiring process needed to allow an army of different people and narratives to tell the story of our past, and most of all our future. Moving demonstrates this: homes do not exist per se. Only homemaking exists: an extended minuet of mutual domestication of people and possessions. A 'home' is an act of self-domestication, performed to make us fit for the world in which we live and, vice versa, it is the domestication of the world to transform the home into a suit, a costume so well cut that it merges with our anatomy and with our image.

This ability to transform ourselves into something connatural with what is around us and, vice versa, to transform something outside ourselves into a thing from which we are inseparable, is perhaps the most intimate of those strengths that typify our life. It's not something that derives from the fact of being human: all creatures have it, and it may be the most basic element of what we call 'life'. It begins with the first breath: compared to our mother's womb, the world is a new home, and we need to take gradual possession of it, to habituate ourselves to it initially through our physical body, whose substance changes on birth.

Ancient Stoic philosophers had suggested calling it *oikeiōsis*, a magnificent word that means 'appropriation' (in the double sense of making something one's own and of making oneself part of something else), 'habituation' (in the double sense of assimilating something to oneself or assimilating oneself into something else), or 'domestication'. The first impulse of a living creature, they wrote, is to look after its own body and its own consciousness, to the extent that it makes it its own.

Opening our eyes, starting to breathe, moving about, building intimacy with what we are, getting used to ourselves – we never stop doing it, and over time we incorporate ever-wider fragments of the world. Homes are only an extended and augmented form of what we begin to do when we breathe and open our eyes for the first time: we build intimacy, assimilate with what is close by, loving what we touch and smoothing it to such an extent that it becomes our skin. Here we must talk about 'building', since intimacy, even with our own selves, is not a given, but an artifice. There again, it's a paradoxical artifice, for it also brings about its own disappearance.

Intimacy is precisely that state in which it is impossible to distinguish between the natural and the artificial; the dizzying wonderment of discovering an entirely new aspect to something that has been with us for years. And from this point of view there is no longer any difference between body and mind. Mind, in the end, represents the effort of bodies to be intimate with all other bodies (to such an extent as to allow them inside us, at least as images and feelings). Intimacy is the true name for what we call 'consciousness' and 'care'.

It's by moving home that I have learned to understand the mental and physical movement we refer to as 'I'. We have reduced the subjectivity of a strange intangible entity, confined in an otherworldly space which, with variable success, we have called 'soul', 'psyche', 'spirit'. For centuries, we were compelled to accept the notion of this entity's incarnation and presence in the anatomy and physiology of our bodies, and yet the 'I' is not a question of soul or of bodies. It is always the movement of the world; it is always the whole planet that says 'I' in each one of us. A home is the 'I', though not as a private and singular fact – of just one subject, or just one body – but as a common vortex that encompasses a series of subjects, a series of things, a place in the world: it is the threshold at which the subject becomes reality in the world, and the world begins to have a single unmistakable face. Every home is only the telluric evidence of the fact that, in order to say 'I', we need a world, a space around us, made up of things, of people who conspire with us, and with those with whom we conspire; the 'I' is this vortex in which, for one instant, bodies and minds seek to habituate themselves to one another.

Every time we move, the 'I' reveals itself for what it is: a catalogue of a possible and shared world – it matters little that it is made up of things or emotions. That is why moving home is sometimes so difficult: it means contemplating everything we require in order to say 'I'. And it's in this moment that we tend to invent ways of shedding parts of the world that no longer belong to us. Still, we could never rid ourselves of the world entirely. We can leave objects, people and affections behind us, but we can never do without domesticating others, habituating ourselves to others: we will become homes once again, even in our most nomadic moments. Living means relocating. It means absorbing a part of the world and being absorbed by it, then allowing it to say 'I' in us.

LOVE

Sometimes, to view it, you had to queue in single file, just as you do at any post office. Sometimes, in Paris, these queues snaked down the whole stairway of grand Haussmann buildings, from the sixth floor to the courtyard, through the main entrance and into the street, ragged and disorganized. Dozens of strangers queuing to visit a tiny student apartment, carrying documents bearing the final proof that here was the chosen one. Having reached the top of the queue, it was hard to shake off a sense of unease and betrayal. I always had the impression I was witnessing something profane. Once through the door it was impossible to feel or imagine any exclusive relationship with what would have to become my home.

Even before we move, our relationship with a new home begins with the strange ritual of the first visit, which varies according to the times, our financial means, and above all the customs and cultures of different countries. Of all possible forms of relationship with a home, this is perhaps the most hypnotic. The deal is often done through an aesthetic judgement on the arrangement and size of rooms, the quantity of light, the quality of the parquet. And yet, the first contact is always an attempt to decipher the promise of shared happiness – a promise made with clues, signals and indications that are heavily veiled and difficult to interpret – through the objects placed there. At this stage, such apparently superficial details – the length of a corridor, type of radiators, shape of the handles, quality of the skirting board – simply introduce what novels call 'real-life touches' into the image of a future life.

In those moments, often imbued with anxiety and embarrassment, we recognize our ability and need to envision our life: to relate to it and to ourselves in a manner that has nothing to do with our own wishes, or with the law, but in much the same way as we relate to the climate in which we live. We view that house in the same way that we see the sky when we wake in the morning; we view it as our sky. In those few minutes, all precepts, catechisms and pious intentions in our moral notions are abandoned, and what is left becomes a superior form of imagination, the only way that we access what we have been and will be.

If such an effort has always been extremely difficult – at least for me – it's because visiting these apartments means being compelled to picture the past inhabitants that have lived and shaped that space. As the years go by, my needs and my financial circumstances have changed, and the queues to view the apartments have gone. I have found myself alone with the estate agent in spaces which are sometimes empty, yet often filled with signs and vestiges of all those lives that have been lived there and then moved on. The moral upheaval has never related to particular details – the sixteenth-century chest of drawers, a Danish lamp or an unmatched teacup – but to the fact that to notice such things has meant suddenly finding myself thrust into someone else's life and being unable to draw a precise boundary between theirs and my own: becoming myself the coffee grounds in which somebody might seek to read a possible future.

When I arrived at one of the four places in which I lived in Berlin, I found some diaries left by a previous tenant. I spent three days deciphering their pages and living a life that wasn't mine. I read them surrounded by the same furniture, curtains and pictures that had not yet been taken down from the walls, which meant transforming myself for an instant into a character in a multi-handed drama. I've often asked myself the uneasy question how my successors in all the domestic universes in which I have lived have viewed my life, or the debris of the life I've left behind. The excitement and sorrow of every apartment always derives from the fact that to imagine my life as home means imagining it indissolubly linked to something else, and above all to other people.

We always talk about the home as private space, the place that separates us from one another and makes us individual. Yet every home is really just the physical and mental material that we use to interweave our life and our destiny with those of others. This is its main purpose, and, for this reason, its nature is not architectural but moral. I repeat, the inadequacy of our homes is never purely architectural or aesthetic but is always and above all ethical. When our homes disappoint us, it's because they cannot maintain the silent promise of shared happiness that they had made at our first meeting. On the other hand, we have lost the ability to imagine homes because we have stopped cultivating the knowledge, the technique, that allows two lives to live one and the same life – what, for centuries, we have called 'love'. Homes are always spatial means of experiencing love in all its manifestations. They are none other than the material blueprint, the framework, but also the objective atmosphere, the climate for a shared life – the time, temperament, food, sleep and dreams that make us inseparable from someone else. It is impossible to consider and construct homes without considering and constructing love.

The opposite is also true: whether it's our home or that of another, or a hotel far away from where we both live, or a country cottage, love is nurtured, cherished and celebrated at home. Indeed, deep down, it's the quintessential domestic mystery, and that is why every city has to claim love for itself through complicated rituals and convoluted legal dispositions. It's impossible to love without setting up home, without involving a piece of the world in an orbit that says 'I' for both of us.

There is nothing natural, obvious or universal

about this equation. It is perhaps the most pro-found, original and idiosyncratic aspect of what the West has called 'modernity'. It was the Canadian philosopher Charles Taylor who recognized that modernity is not only the result of technological development, of European dominance over other parts of the globe, or of transformations in society and forms of government: at its centre there is a revolutionary moral project that has brought every-day life, defined by love and labour – its most ordinary and trivial features – to the centre of every political, economic, social and material concern. We are modern not because we use sophisticated technological devices, because we can travel to every part of the planet or because we live in over-crowded cities. We are modern because we claim that our identity is defined in what we produce and what we do freely each day, and in whom we love. We are modern only when we think that freedom and moral perfection are measured in the freedom to love and to work. No other culture ever imag-ined such a thing.

And if work has become both the foundation and the centre of the city, the home – released from the need to be the site of production – has instead become the temple of love, of the daily symbiotic relationship with another person. It's no surprise that all the great moral revolutions to which we ascribe an idea of progress are linked to the improvement of work conditions and the freedom to love. And yet while nations involved in the process of modernization have given much thought over the past two centuries to work – its dignity, its form and its preconditions – love still needs to find a form of legitimacy in public as well as academic debate.

Apart from one area of sociology and of feminism, love in all its manifestations continues to be considered a minor, frivolous, secondary subject (who would ever dare to think of work as something that so-called 'women's magazines' should concern themselves with?) or a matter for priests, moralists and psychoanalysts. The problem with this imbalance is the real reason why the project of modernity cannot be fully achieved. Our modernity has always been incomplete and malformed precisely because we have neglected one of the mainstays of daily life, the centre of the modern moral project. And in a context in which work seems increasingly incapable of defining our identity (certainly not in economic terms), the lack of consideration given to love makes any incarnation of modernity literally impossible. We cannot succeed in being modern, because we haven't yet learned to love.

This cultural taboo is rooted in the sexism of our civilization: historically, knowledge about the love relation – not just and not necessarily in its erotic form, but in every way – was the common and exclusive domain of women, who for millennia (and still today) have been systematically excluded from culture, science and public life. The consequences of this exclusion are dramatic. Not only is love not considered to be a subject worthy of study (whereas work is, in all its forms), but none of us regard love as something that requires application and commitment. It's an area of existence that is immediately connected to amusement, to distraction. And that's why it has become the subject of farces and drawing-room comedies.

While Eros has been downgraded to a minor divinity, Heracles enjoys cult status. Parity between them seems impossible – in the freedom each supposes, in the results to be expected, in the belief that a fulfilled life is possible. Try reversing the rhetoric used in public discussions of work and love: try transferring all pleas for sacrifice and self-denial to love, and all calls for the need to be free to work. Why is work alone taken seriously? Why is freedom the sole prerogative of love?

It's as though, to quote Stendhal's famous distinction (repeated a few decades ago by the Italian sociologist Francesco Alberoni) between falling in love and love itself, contemporary society had concentrated solely on falling in love, on the nascent state of harmony and encounter, but not on the real, the effective, and – most importantly – the lasting relationship.

The fact that even technological progress has focused only on this stage, with the rise of dating apps such as Tinder, Bumble, Grindr, and their variants, is a further demonstration of this. We can do without thinking about homes precisely because we experience love only to experience falling in love.

For the same reason, while architectural reflection on the city has reached unprecedented levels of complexity, and contemporary urban reality has a brilliance incomparable to the past, the thought given to the home, and above all to building practices for the ordinary domestic environment, is so crude and prehistoric that it still allows the vast majority of architects to believe that the problem posed by each house is one of the spatial composition of a few rectangles that have each been given some vital purpose: sleep for the bedroom, entertainment for the sitting room, eating for the kitchen. The futurist imagination practised for centuries over the city has never touched on private dwellings. It's for this reason that every home gives the impression that the horizon of moral possibility is shrinking rather than expanding, that it's necessary to adapt our life to crude Euclidean geometry which, for inexplicable reasons, is considered the key to a happy and successful existence. When we walk into homes today, instead of experiencing a liberating sense of emotional and moral modernity, we can only feel the crudeness of our moral imagination.

But the difficulty in conceiving love – and therefore the home – is not just due to the fragility and moral blindness of our culture. Love, in the end, is the black hole of every moral reflection due to its very structure. It is the ethical space in which life can rely on no precept, no law, no certainty – but not because it's an anarchic dimension outside the law. On the contrary, there's nothing more structured than the experience of love. It is, however, a special structure. In antiquity, these forms of morality were generally called 'mysteries': dimensions of existence which could be accessed neither through knowledge nor through law, but through rites of initiation alone.

'Mystery' in this context does not mean something unknown. After all, countless realities are unfamiliar to us, yet almost none is a mystery. The overwhelming majority of faces we pass as we walk along the street of any modern city are unfamiliar, and yet they rarely hold any mystery for us. Nor do we find this quality in the many thousands of books arranged along the shelves of a library. Mystery doesn't just refer to that which is extraneous to our knowledge; it is something that is resistant to understanding and above all to our desire. For this very reason, access to this sphere can only be achieved through initiation: it requires a third party who will allow us to experience this reality. Mystery is a way of being which can be accessed only through the life of the Other; for this very reason it is utterly unknowable, and for this very reason the order of desire in this life will never be freed from fear. The knowledge that generally makes it possible to overcome fear is, in the case of mystery, technically unachievable. Love is the transcendental form of this experience.

Every home ought, in the end, to be the structure that allows one life to live through the Other: not an envelope of glass, steel and cement that separates us from the rest of the world, nor the window of variable geometry that enables us to make our own 'I' visible, especially to ourselves, but the mental and physical quest of mutual initiation between lives. A home should be the secular, worldly embodiment of mystery.

3

BATHROOMS

Towards the end of the last century (a strange thing to be saying, but true), I had just moved to Berlin and was living in a metropolis for the first time. It was very cold, but very bright. The city was living through a confused but exciting interregnum. The fall of the Wall had freed it from division and from the Communist regime; it had been chosen as the capital of a reunified Germany. The parliament hadn't yet arrived, nor had the panoply of offices and bureaucrats that would come with it and transform the city into something much more monitored and ordered than it would naturally be. The streets and houses exuded a sense of euphoria, short-lived yet intense: people here, in East Berlin, lived in a way that was different from elsewhere; it seemed possible to imagine an alternative life for the whole continent.

Here I could rent a 60-square-metre apartment

for the same as I would have paid for a bed in the hall of residence of a provincial Italian university town. People dressed differently: Berlin in the late 1990s, without realizing it, was the testing ground for what would later become the New York hipster style. The inhabitants ate differently, and generally quite badly. Above all, homes differed in their furnishings, style and layout. The most surprising feature was the lack of a bathroom in many East Berlin apartments. Toilets had been built on the half-landings of stairwells since the end of the nineteenth century, and the reason for this was not just economic. An order from the city's building regulators on 15 January 1887 had decreed that bathrooms had to have access to natural light and air, and the structure, design and layout of large buildings for the working classes didn't always allow that. The landing was therefore the solution adopted.

These spaces were invariably tiny – like the toilets I would find years later in Paris, except that those had no windows or ventilation – and lacked any elements to distract the bodies that frequented them from the mechanical execution of the purpose for which they had been designed. Their stark character was not the symptom of an early and involuntary adherence to the functionalist model of architectural modernism. In such enclosed places, with no heating and in a city where winter temperatures frequently dropped to 10 or 15 degrees below zero, to linger any longer than strictly necessary, far from offering any prospect of idle pleasure, was more a test of thermal resilience. During the nineteenth century, such hardships were avoided by using bedroom commodes. But in the Berlin nights of the late twentieth century, going to the bathroom was like an Antarctic expedition, and to survive that open-air refrigerator the lack of adequate heating required an improvised protection consisting of three or four sweaters and several layers of velvet trousers to cope with the icy conditions outside my apartment door.

This continued spatial exile was not connected to the frequent and quite usual separation in Paris between one space for physiological purification (*salle de toilette*) and one for bodily hygiene (*salle de bain*). No rooms in these apartments were set apart for bodily care. With the end of the Communist regime and the first wave of modernization, rather than totally rebuilding the apartments, the toilets were left on the half-landings and attempts were made to cater for the new bathing customs of the population by installing showers in the only domestic space that could satisfy their technical requirements – the kitchen.

I had a shower too. Beside the sink, the oven, the dishwasher, and shelves holding packs of pasta, spices and olive oil, was a large Perspex cabin for my bodily hygiene. A small detail, yet it was enough to transform the whole apartment into a surreal dream: those practices that would generally have led me to the privacy of the bathroom came perilously close to those others that exposed my body to friends in the kitchen. The action of mixing flavours and aromas of creatures of other kinds in that zoo and garden of metamorphosis which is a kitchen became inseparable from the effort to keep my body human and clean. There was something explosive in the attempt to make bodily hygiene and gastronomic desire coexist. After all, when Luis Buñuel sought to invert bourgeois moral codes in *The Phantom of Liberty*, he simply reversed the logic that applies to the toilet and the kitchen, making the act of defecation something public, while eating became a private act to be performed secluded in a kind of toilet.

He had never thought of connecting them on a spatial and gestural level.

The effect wasn't always pleasant, and yet it was this experience that made me realize what the rooms of a home are. A bathroom and kitchen weren't just two separate rectangles in the layout of the apartments in which I had lived. They were two imaginations, two universes morally distinct and barely reconcilable. The confused layout of their spaces and their volumes caused me to rethink the way I lived, but also my ideas and the feelings I experienced each time I was at home. It's in the short-circuit produced by this chimera – the *bathroom-kitchen* – that I realized how designing a home means subjecting those who live there to a precise mental planimetry: organizing their feelings, their emotions, the form of their experience. And the bathroom, which we generally associate with the more bodily functions of our daily life, is also and above all the heart of domestic psychagogy.

We come from an architectural tradition that has sought to imagine and adapt living space to the human being in strictly anatomical terms. This tradition is more generally that which has always considered technical artefacts as an extension of the human body and of certain organs. The German philosopher Ernst Kapp was the first to give a clear formulation of this idea in 1877. 'Man', he wrote, 'unconsciously projects the form, the functional relationship and normal rapport of his bodily organization onto the workings of his hand and becomes aware only *après coup* of this analogous relationship.' It is this projection, this 'extension of itself towards externality', that makes it possible 'to render nature intelligible and to make use of it', but also 'for man to express his own being'. It is through technical manipulation that mankind understands the world in which it lives. This organic projection is therefore the condition for every human activity. It's as though, to inhabit this world, we had to reshape it in our physical image, in our anatomical likeness.

This same intuition drove modern architecture to relate the form and design of living spaces to the anatomical proportions of the body that inhabited them. The most radical example of this approach is Le Corbusier's Modulor, the mathematical and geometrical model that enabled him to design and construct his *unité d'habitation*. The Modulor – a composite word from *module* and *nombre d'or* – follows and modifies the Renaissance scheme of the Vitruvian man: it represents an individual with one raised arm that illustrates the proportionate dimensions of the human body and projects them onto the external space. 'A house', wrote Le Corbusier, 'is a machine for living in': 'baths, sun, hot water, cold water, warmth at will, conservation of food, hygiene, beauty in the sense of good proportion'.[1] It is therefore only by adopting the model of bodily projection that a home can be designed like this, in the same way that a pen, a pencil, a telephone, a razor, a car, a motorboat, an aeroplane, or 'an armchair' (which is 'a machine for sitting in') are designed using the outline of the body that will use them. Indeed, for Le Corbusier, this conformity between architectural artefacts and human anatomy has always existed.

'The Parthenon,' he wrote, 'the temples of India and the cathedrals were built according to precise measures constituting a code, a coherent system that asserted an essential unity', that of the human body. The proof, he argued, lies in the fact that the same units for measuring space take their name from the forms of the human anatomy (digit, inch, foot, cubit, span), thereby reducing the world to an extension of our body. This happened because the instruments 'were an integral part of the human body, and thus fit to serve as measures for the huts, houses and temples that had to be built'. Their effectiveness depended on their uniformity with the body of the person who inhabited such spaces: these were instruments 'infinitely rich and subtle because they formed part of the mathematics of the human body, graceful, elegant and firm, the source of that harmony which moves us, beauty'. This is so for physiological reasons: 'man occupies the space to govern it according to his needs' and 'he occupies it through his members: his legs, his trunk, his arms, outstretched or raised. He bends at the solar plexus, lynchpin of its movements'. This 'strangely simple' mechanism is based on the fact that 'it is the only setting for our behaviour, our taking possession of space': 'a piece of machinery or furniture, a newspaper are extensions of human gestures'.

And yet precisely for this reason we should recognize that to enable, prolong or modify the form of a gesture simply means modifying the psychology that sustains it. A home is a mental sculpture, a kind of spatialization of our mind and gesturalization of the body – its translation into gestures, habits and feelings. Each of its elements is a machinery that influences our mind much more than our body because it educates our feelings, our emotions, our imagination following a specific order that we hardly notice. The bathroom is perhaps the clearest proof.

The spaces that make up an apartment resemble ancient concubines. As years go by, the habits, ideas, opinions, sighs and pleasures of old lovers overlap so much that each of their bodies seems to slip into the flesh of the other and inhabit the life of both indistinctively. Likewise, though their cubic spaces cannot merge, the rooms of a house occupied for a long while each echo the other until they seem to breathe with a single breath. Each seems to be disguised as the other in spite of the walls, the doors, the essential differences of furniture – and of the living functions they accommodate.

In this drift towards the liquefaction of spaces and atmospheres, there is one room – the bathroom – which resists the overall symbiosis and amalgamation. In every house, this room is the expression and incarnation of an unyielding difference or, rather, of an obstinate urge for extraneity. Every bathroom is the architectural expression of an intolerable domestic dandyism: a space-time that refuses to merge with others, to mix itself up with others, to admit that the life that goes on inside its walls can also take place outside. And it's not just a question of physical separation or geometrical isolation. This room, which we might think belongs obviously and naturally to the very idea of home, was the last to form part of it, modelling itself on bathrooms in American hotels at the beginning of the twentieth century. Yet in doing so, it offered something to the private daily life of individuals – bodily care with liquid, steam, cleanliness, ablutions – which had, however, a more general implication.

To concentrate in a confined space something that would usually have a major impact on an area's hydrogeological balance, it was necessary to resort to a radical form of mechanization. The bathroom, along with the kitchen, is the most technically complex and therefore most modern space in every home because it involves a hidden circulation of elements that are not found elsewhere. Its physical and chemical composition requires it. The bathroom has characteristics that differ from the rest of the home. A house consists mainly of air and stone, but the bathroom is, by definition, a place in which liquids dominate, whether they are toxic wastes to be discharged or liquids that revive and refresh.

This is also why bathrooms still flaunt quite another style in their aesthetic identity: they are the only rooms that can afford to have an appearance which bears no resemblance to the rest of the home – in materials, colours and decoration.

Its obstinate difference depends also on the rigorous functionalist doctrine that every bathroom must follow. In other domestic spaces, some margin is permitted between form and purpose – a kitchen is often a workplace, the bedroom a study area, a corridor a space where children play. A bathroom is physically and spiritually defined by one single function. On the other hand, when it is pushed outside those domestic confines, a surreal effect is hard to avoid.

The bathroom embodies an impossible logic of detachment and synthesis. If every home represents a separate sphere, the bathroom is a home inside the home: an inner sanctum, a bolted room. Here is the absolute protection of an environment in which we feel an urge to be safe. If it is unwilling or incapable of being assimilated physically, architecturally and aesthetically with the rest of the house, this is because it's a kind of moral sentinel stationed in almost every home throughout the world: its most intimate intention is to filter out certain experiences, to separate certain bodily gestures. Every house is an alembic through which we distil our most private and personal life, controlling the access and presence of others. The bathroom is the alembic within the alembic that distils something even more private, an intimacy in which no one else is ever expected to be involved. It is no surprise that this is the only room into which we normally lock ourselves, as well as the only room where we run the risk of getting locked in. It's the guardian of an implacable moral universe, the setting for something that is impossible elsewhere in the house. This physical and spiritual ghettoization produces a tragic victim as collateral damage: Eros.

The bathroom represents abject shame, a place of embarrassment and guilt, which clears the stage for the discovery of gender, that fragile relationship each one of us must invent each day with our own sexual organ. It was behind the locked door of the bathroom at home that I tried to grasp the first secrets of the pleasures of Eros so as not to be discovered even by my brother, with whom a strange pact of silence reigned. And I remember men's changing rooms, those places so near to hell, shared bathrooms in which maybe the worst consequences of the ideology of mentally ghettoizing Eros emerge, of which bathrooms are a symptom. Separating us as individuals or by gender, compelling the 'male' and 'female' to contend with their organs of Eros in absolute solitude, bathrooms have produced the worst misunderstandings about the body and about the possibility of using it to produce pleasure for ourselves and for others.

Sexual organs are perhaps the oddest of all the organs we possess. They're the only ones whose use presupposes the presence of another person. Whether it's a question of obtaining pleasure or attempting to reproduce, we need to get there through the use of another's body or their image. It is always another hand that gives us pleasure; it is always another body that we use to obtain bliss and gratification. This happens with no other organ: we use our hands, eyes, mouth, feet, heart and nose with no need for anyone else – at least from the time we learn to walk. With sexual organs, on the other hand, it's as though we are constantly in a situation of minority or disadvantage. They are imperfect organs: they don't make us more perfect but less complete, less defined, less 'ourselves' than any other portion of our anatomy. It's only the fictitious setting of solitude created by bathrooms that fools us into thinking these organs can give us some desperate identity.

Every species carves its own silhouette, and each new anatomical function is accompanied by a greater independence, a greater determination. Sexual organs, however, have the task of softening our contours and making us more indeterminate. It's not just a question of shape, but one of awareness. These instruments are also mystical, in the literal sense of the word: a penis and a vagina are organs that we can only know and to which we can only properly be initiated through the bodies of others; even when we are alone, we pretend or imagine that we are with another person. That is why the sexual organ doesn't define an identity but a gender: in front of it we are never alone and can never be alone. We can use it and get to know it only through others and, vice versa, that part of our anatomy serves above all to get to know and to use the body of another. In this respect the sexual organ is the opposite of an organ of perception.

Sex equates to gender because it is a way of experiencing, knowing and inhabiting other bodies, and for being known and manipulated by them. It's from this particular state of affairs that all the painful paradoxes of Eros originate.

By compelling our body to become 'gendered' – generic, indeterminable in life, belonging no more to us than to those who can use it to produce pleasure for themselves and for others – the sex organ removes our existence from the immediate, direct knowledge to which we are accustomed thanks to the awareness produced by the senses and by the brain. By means of gender – life with sexuality and therefore a life knowable only through the use that others can make of it – our body stops belonging to us on a physical and a cognitive level. We are necessarily obliged to overlap with and allow ourselves to be overlapped by the pleasures of others, with all the risks and unexpected discoveries that this can bring. Sex – gender – is what makes every form of identity impossible and every form of assertion of it ridiculous.

There is no single gender identity: in every gender there are at least two components, and their interaction is always in the way of an experiment, a temporary bid. Gender is not, and can never be, something that allows us to be different from others: it transforms us into a moral sphinx. A sphinx is a fanciful composition of two bodies: gender brings together in a temporary collage two bodies joined only by pleasure and mutual good; it's a place of mystery for both. This is also why it's impossible to build a scientific learning on Eros: around the sphinx there can only be enigma. The morality of gender is always a collective work, for which a tradition is impossible: it can never rely on the past, and, insofar as it is bound to a use which will always be that of someone else, it can never be regulated by precepts. In gender there is always only divination.

For almost two centuries we have been accustomed to thinking that it's through labour that we acquire universality: Karl Marx explained that we are generic beings (*Gattungswesen*) only because we can relate freely and consciously to the life of the species. And yet, even before acting, before transforming the world, we build our happiness by copulating. Because of our sex – and it matters little what form it takes – we are bodies in which other bodies know the key that leads to happiness and well-being. Due to our penises and our vaginas, we are desires that need to be seized and manipulated by subjects other than those expressed in our 'I'.

This universal is something much more fragile and ephemeral than that built by labour. And bathrooms, much more than alienated labour, are what make this construction more difficult. To free gender, to free homes from the logic of confinement that every bathroom embodies, means making it the space in which each body intersects with other bodies, and is intersected by them. A space that the next occupant will always be able to open and understand.

4

HOUSEHOLD ARTICLES

I was at Freiburg, in southern Germany. I had just obtained my first job. I was to teach the history of medieval and ancient philosophy at the university, doing research along the same lines, and assisting the professor to run faculty life. As soon as I arrived, I began looking for somewhere to live. For the first time, I could do so without worrying about how much the apartment cost and could focus on its appearance. I found one that was open-plan – enormous in comparison to those I'd had before – in a recently finished building. But I chose it, really, for the magnificent red porthole which transformed the kitchen area into a space-station hovering in the sky.

The owner was the building's architect. He invited me to complete the formalities by signing the rental contract in his office a few hours after my visit. It was early afternoon and within a few minutes I had the keys. Then, as if to compensate for my excessive good fortune, my credit card stopped working. It was impossible to figure out why, but I was still in good spirits: I had a roof over my head and enough cash to eat – badly – for at least a week.

The only problem was that the apartment was totally empty. It had nothing: no bed, no mattress, no chair, not even a plate or a fork. Nothing. None of the objects that populate our homes or hotel rooms. I had imagined going to live in a spacecraft and found myself in the emptiness of space itself. I hadn't enough money to start furnishing it, nor to stay in a hotel, and knew no one in the city, so I lived for a week in a Platonic ideal of space instead of an actual home.

It was my most important experience of recent years. During those days I realized that space in its geometrical purity is physically uninhabitable. I had a home in which the most basic act of living was impossible. It was impossible to sleep because the floor was too hard and too cold: to do so I needed blankets, a pillow, pyjamas and above all a mattress. I needed things, not space. Even working there was impossible: I needed a table, a chair, a computer and a work light – things. Eating was impossible, too: I couldn't cook without cooking pots. It was impossible to deal with food using just my hands, with no knives, forks or spoons. Above all, it was impossible to stay there for long: the contemplation of emptiness is dreadful, unbearable, deafening.

The home in terms of form – its ground, roof and walls – is really, by definition, uninhabitable. It's an abstraction because, instead of being constructed on the reality of acts and the world of objects and feelings that populate each of our lives, it reduces them to something exclusively geometrical. In reality, from a moral point of view, space does not exist. We never meet it. We inhabit a world always populated by other human beings, by every kind of plant, animal and object. And these objects are not an extension of our environment; they don't just occupy space, instead they open it, they make it possible. The bed, plates, table, computer and fridge all give reality to a dimension that is otherwise only imaginary and abstract, a pure mental projection in which it is literally forbidden to enter and impossible to occupy. Indeed, we occupy only things. Objects are what accommodate our body, our gestures; they attract our attention, prevent us from colliding with the perfectly angular geometrical surfaces of the home and protect us from its violence. The home as a box, from a technical point of view, is a form of desert, a purely mineral structure.

It was this experience that taught me that the domestic space does not have a Euclidean nature. The movements of my body at home do not follow the geometry I studied at school. The things that occupy our apartments are not extensions of our anatomy; they are magnets, attractors, sirens that bend and seduce the reality of domestic space with irresistible melodies and transform it into a field of constantly unstable forces, a network of sensitive influences that free us only once we have closed the front door behind us. That is why we feel tired on those days when we go outside less than usual. Staying at home means having to resist all the forces that these objects exert on each other, and on us. Life at home is resistance – in an electric, not a mechanical sense. We are a tungsten filament crossed by the force of objects. We light up or switch off thanks to them.

Where does this force come from? I understood only much later, and it was my daughter who taught me this. It comes from us. If objects come alive each time we walk through the front door, it's because they acquire a part of us. Clothing, pieces of paper on which we've noted down a number or doodled while phoning a friend, a painting, our daughter's toy – they exist as though they were subjects, egos with forms unlike that human form, which look at us and talk to us. Through use, through the daily routines that stretch over days, months and years, the friction of our bodies on their bodies leaves traces, it magnetizes them, it transfers a part of our personality onto them. All objects in the home become subjects. Here's a good definition: home is that space in which all objects exist as subjects. It's the exact opposite of slavery. It's the place in which things stop being things: a panpsychic machine of universal animation, a mechanism which reveals that inside everything there's an 'I', a space of involuntary animism. And we don't always realize it.

On alternate weeks, my daughter, a skilled shaman and expert animist, teaches me to open the doors of perception. My days are then populated with presences very different from those biologically definable as 'living beings'. Colette doesn't just share her time, her games, her tastes, her little idiosyncrasies. She guides me into her universe, which is inhabited by all kinds of characters whose stories aren't always easy to figure out. Some are naturally more important: Ladybug, an adolescent who turns into a girl-ladybird with incredible powers (her favourite); Akko, a small gawky witch who reveals magical secrets hidden in the Arcturus Forest (my favourite); She-Ra, a warrior princess who can save the planet Etheria; and the Octonauts, a curious band of sea creatures who travel the universe to save the most unlikely living species.

Most of the other presences, however, seem to enjoy a much more fragile, ephemeral, intangible existence. Like all children her age – she is five-and-a-half – my daughter is a great animist: for her, the world is made up not of objects but of an infinite iridescence of subjects, souls and presences. She can therefore recognize a form of consciousness in the smallest piece of paper that vaguely resembles a human figure, but also has the sensitivity to understand that her dolls and her fluffy toys are inhabited each week by different personalities. Not only their names, but also their personal histories and their family relationship to her change regularly and need to be recognized immediately.

One day my daughter invited one of her imaginary friends for dinner. These, for me, are the most difficult to recognize since they are souls without a body. I may have reacted discourteously to their lively girlish conversations that excluded the adult at the table. Without batting an eyelid, Colette turned and explained what was going on: 'Don't worry, papa,' she assured me, 'it's quite normal for you not to see her, and she can't see you either.' At that moment I lost all my scepticism. And a thought flashed through my mind. It was, for me, the final proof that what I believed to be a 'childish' attitude was nothing naive and primitive: my daughter's animism was a kind of complex, subtle and above all reflective awareness. We tend to think that this kind of behaviour disappears with age – once reason takes over our life. And yet nothing is certain anymore. Most of all today.

When my daughter is at school, I spend my days in front of a strange object made of polymers, plastic, ceramic, copper, iron, nickel and silicon. I spend a lot of time talking to it. Sometimes hours. This object very often responds. It does so in a very articulate and often boring way, in different languages. Unlike the nineteenth century, which gave the name 'spiritualism' to this kind of experiment, we prefer to talk more soberly about 'Zoom sessions'. We prefer not to admit it, but computers or mobile phones are machines that turn animism into an ordinary commonplace experience. During our WhatsApp calls or Zoom meetings we don't see a computer or a telephone. We see souls, subjects and consciousnesses encapsulated in a body that is not biological. It would be naive to reply that what these machines really give us are signs or representation. Words or images are independent – in time and in being – of what they represent. The presences that infest my computer or my telephone are not. For long hours the metallic object is visited and plagued by various consciousnesses. Technology has filled objects with spirit. There's nothing particularly disturbing about this sort of cyberanimism. It merely extends the domestic way of existing to all artefacts; it's for this very reason that a telephone or a computer are domestic objects even when they are physically outside the confines of our apartments. The material in them comes alive just as it does inside the home.

Since the end of the nineteenth century, anthropology has used the term 'animism' to characterize the way of thinking of certain cultures for whom particular objects – first and foremost fetishes, namely artefacts that represent gods – are considered to have qualities generally recognized as exclusively human, namely personality, consciousness and even the ability to act. Our own culture has always claimed to be a stranger to this kind of thinking: we have absolute faith in the clear and inevitable separation between things and people, between objects and subjects. And yet we tolerate animistic relationships with a much vaster number of objects than dolls. In a posthumous book published twenty years ago, a great English anthropologist, Alfred Gell, defended a surprising and counter-intuitive proposition: we call 'art' the sphere in which we, in the West, allow things to have an existence almost parallel to human existence. Just think what happens in a museum: millions of people spend hours contemplating pieces of matter – linen covered with pigments, wood, bronze, marble, lead – convinced that they understand in them the thoughts, attitudes and feelings of a person who they have never met and about whom they know nothing. Most of them even demonstrate their readiness to speculate keenly on the psychological particulars of the minds that haunt these objects. They refuse to obey common sense: instead of granting spirit only to beings anatomically identical to us, they insist they can see intentions and ideas in a block of marble or bronze, and claim these objects speak to them. Museums are not spaces in which we accumulate objects that stir feelings of aesthetic admiration and pleasure; they are temples of an unconscious collective animist cult, which allow us to worship objects and recognize that in portions of matter that have no biological life there exists a soul akin to ours.

Homes are private sanctuaries for this same secret cult. They are personal museums that allow us to discover and contemplate our soul while it lives outside our body, while it circulates and breathes in each of the objects that surround us, even the most insignificant, even the least attractive. It lives in all our clothes and in the washing machine that periodically resurrects them; it lives in the chairs and in the beds that save us from moving; in the books and the worlds contained inside them; in the pictures that decorate the walls; in the curtains that shut out the light; in the carpets we trample without too much thought; and in the coffee machine that saves us each morning. Household objects are extensions of our body simply because they are animated by the same life that gives life to it. And each household object not only contains a part of us, but also becomes an earlier version of our ego. Our embarrassment around animism compels us to consider this relationship in the rather crude terms of private property or, at other times, in those equally coarse aspects of decoration and interior design. And yet arriving home means always abandoning the Cartesian universe comprised of intangible minds and a boundless expanse of inanimate matter. A home is a space-time curvature where the tiniest portion of matter says 'I' and, vice versa, where personality, emotions, memory and sense render subjects and objects indistinguishable. We need to build homes to give life to objects and to draw from them all the soul that our body cannot produce and accommodate. This is what we try to grasp each time we imagine the presence of ghosts and spectres: a home is no more than the clearest, most disturbing symptom of the fact that the mind can live everywhere and circulates freely from human beings to objects and from objects to human beings.

5

WARDROBES

The first apartment I lived in was just a few steps from the sea. The first picture of that place that comes to mind is the silhouette of three enormous umbrella pines a few hundred metres from the balcony of the bedroom I shared with my brother. They stood there, as though rooted to the ground for ever. They stood there, between me and the horizon, blocking the view, screening every other perception of the world as if they were its custodians and at the same time its guides. Like three Titans in charge of the cosmos. Like three Dioscuri or three Graces destined to protect my every step and follow my gaze. They seemed to embody the Platonic form of those umbrella pines that Félix Vallotton immortalized in his famous painting *Last Rays* (or *Landscape with Trees*) (1911), or those seen in any postcard depicting the Mediterranean coast, or those that give the gardens of Rome and the surrounding countryside that timeless and sacred appearance of places exempt from human destiny. Their trunks were thin and slightly bent, their bark reddish and deeply fissured, and only high up did their branches – like all adult examples of the species – begin to produce a large, rounded crown in the shape of an open umbrella. For years those three lanky trees were my model for an elegant trick of light.

The attic was right above our bedroom. It was a kind of second apartment, at least as big as ours, not occupied by people but filled with the strangest and most unlikely objects. There was, for example, an enormous unfinished picture of Christ and the Apostles painted by my father in his youth, a freezer at least three times my size, old furniture, toys I couldn't figure out, work tools, but above all an indescribable number of clothes. It was a gloomy place, had very little light and I don't think I set foot in many of its rooms. It was a place I didn't much like: I went there only when I had to put something in the freezer or take something out of it.

But there was an additional force that obliged me to spend long hours in those closed windowless spaces: my sister. One of her favourite pastimes, for years, was to stage *tableaux vivants* featuring my brother and me, who were regularly abducted and forced to transform ourselves into living dolls that performed appalling and senseless fashion shows with all the clothes kept up there. During those hours, everything was transfigured according to a logic that I found incomprehensible, and I remember the feeling of exhaustion from the whirl of faces I had to impersonate, and the amazement I felt each time, on leaving at the 'end of the performance', when I found the same darkness outside that reigned in the attic. Above all, I have never forgotten the thrill I felt at being the 'I' who allowed these perpetually dormant creatures, the occupants of this strange apartment, to come back to life and find a new soul.

Attics, like cellars, are cemeteries for household objects: places waiting for an improbable resurrection, places of incarceration in which almost every object is serving a life sentence. In domestic topography, however, wardrobes are exactly the opposite. Not only are all their contents regularly brought out, but concealed inside them are those portable portions of the home specially made for navigating the non-domestic space: clothes. Clothes are ferries, boats, caravans. They don't need wheels because they cling to our bodies. We use them to travel through the world. Thanks to clothes, the home stretches beyond its walls; it continues into a sort of mobile extraterritoriality which follows every minimal movement of our body with infinite precision. Thanks to clothes, in effect, we never leave home; we carry it around with us, we transform it into a kind of second skin. Thanks to clothes, homes are transformed from immense containers into sleek and supple vehicles through which we shelter from the world. On the other hand, with clothes – the mobile extrusions of home – homes stop being a private, invisible space and become a public spectacle, constantly on the move, an individual presence that constantly changes appearance.

That is why clothing and home cannot be considered separately. An item of clothing is a home put into a showcase that allows its content to be seen beyond its own confines, and a home is an item of clothing that has been enlarged to such an extent that it becomes a wardrobe of the mind that nurtures all the transformations of the person who wears it. We enter a home in the same way that we enter our clothes; we inhabit our home in the same way that we inhabit our clothes. What a home does to our body and our soul is much the same as the effect clothes have on us. A home is not just the space in which things become subjects. It is also the place in which all things become extensions of our subjectivity. That's why we need to define clothing and fashion to understand what a house is: each item of clothing, unlike any other artefact, is specially created to allow subjectivity to exist in a certain manner. Through fashion, we are endlessly redesigning our idea of domesticity. Every garment designed and stitched together is the material expression of personal comfort in a place that is not the bedroom, the bathroom or the kitchen: it's an idea of happiness that has become inseparable from our body, that can follow it everywhere. It's thanks to clothing that we can understand how the home always has at least two bodies: one moveable and one immovable, one mineral and one more malleable, one made of pure inwardness and the other of pure outwardness. Home and fashion converge more and more, and the fortunes of one will be connected more and more to those of the other.

Contrary to what people think, today's fashion regime is not a simple contemporary updating – in industrial and aesthetic terms – of the system of sartorial custom that went before it and has always been a part of human history. Today's fashion is not a mere expression of the fact that we dress differently according to local culture, or to ethnic or religious identity, or to protect ourselves from bad weather. And it's not even due simply to the variation of individual taste in dress. Our current fashion regime began when clothing ceased to make an indelible link between the person wearing it and a particular social class. It began when variations of taste were no longer passing accidents of an aesthetic whose sole purpose was to express the financial and cultural superiority of one part of the population over the rest, but instead had to suggest the invention of a new way of being that was potentially accessible to anyone, regardless of their class or financial status. When Coco Chanel invented her *silhouette neuve* which borrowed styles and textiles from male fashion, she wasn't producing yet another opportunity for ostentatious consumption. She was offering a different identity: a woman free from the constraints of a particular role, who could go to work and play sports. Homes should do the same thing: they should invent moral identities.

From this point of view, fashion begins only when the system of production and packaging of clothing consciously adopts the programme of the early twentieth-century art avant-garde: that of making art resemble life. Clothing lends itself particularly well as an embodiment of the total artwork: it's an artefact that all individuals need to have and use, regardless of their class, their financial means, their religion, their sexual orientation or their ideology. And it's something that everyone uses throughout their life – all day, every day, even at night. Unlike other artefacts produced to perfection, it is not used for furnishing the spaces in which we live or the rooms of a museum: we put it on our body and use it as a sort of amulet, as well as a kind of vehicle that carries us everywhere and mediates our social and physical interactions with ourselves and with others. Through clothing, art exists everywhere, at any time, on our skin. Through clothing, art becomes what we are immersed in, not some object of aesthetic contemplation. It's our essential space, and at the same time it's the means by which we perceive the world and ourselves and allow others to perceive us; it's the medium for the construction of experience – experience of whatever kind. That is why fashion, more than any other artistic experience, has been the perfect Trojan horse for introducing art into the daily life of all human beings at every geographical and cultural latitude. More than a discrete artistic skill, fashion has been the place in which all arts are mixed and brought together to transfigure our bodies and our lives.

Fashion is therefore the attempt to make art the medium and the form for the establishment of self. It is not a secondary aspect of the cultural life of contemporary society: it is the extreme expression of the democratic idea of distribution of power among all individuals; it is the assertion that identity in a democratic space is not an a priori fact but is an object of mutual negotiation and construction. It is what was originally expressed in the concept of lifestyle. Introduced into sociology by Georg Simmel and Max Weber and into psychology by Alfred Adler, the idea of lifestyle has nothing to do with any form of aesthetic representation of existence. It is the structure which emerges in those societies that prevent individual lives from being determined by any form of identity, whether biological or ethnic, religious or economic, cultural or sexual. Simmel has demonstrated the true moral project of modern capitalism: the affirmation of money as the means for constructing the whole of society frees the individual from inherited social structures such as class, ethnic origin or religion.

The modern individual can thus oppose these forms of identity with one produced and built on a psychological, cultural and moral basis. Identity is therefore an artefact, a technical and artistic construction. Precisely because it is the product of artifice, it is the consequence of a freely chosen act – and the notion of style expresses this. For if 'style', as Ernst Gombrich wrote, 'is any distinctive, and therefore recognizable, way in which an act is performed or an artefact made or ought to be performed and made', it is also true that 'there can be no question of style unless [there is] the possibility of choosing between alternative forms of expression'.[2]

As a technique that can transform identity into a product, every item of clothing makes identity the expression of a free choice more than of an inherent nature. We are not what we have inherited (nationality, ethnic origin, culture, language) but what we have decided to be and can stop being at any moment. Fashion, from this point of view, is the opposite of custom in a moral sense. In Ancient Rome, the purpose of custom was the reproduction and stability of ancestral morality (*mos maiorum*). Fashion, on the contrary, has to mobilize all customs and morals. The rules embodied in fashion constantly revolutionize morals and modes of dressing, and correspond with a *mos novissimorum*, a sort of paradoxical tradition (*mos* in Latin means 'morals' and 'tradition' as well as 'custom'), that must be constantly updated and where the only fixed element is a trend towards the new. In this sense it's the exact opposite of Roman censure: instead of 'punishing new misdeeds and reviving old customs' (*'castigare* [. . .] *nova flagitia et priscos revocare mores'*),[3] it aims to punish old misdeeds and advocate new customs (*'priscos castigare mores et novos advocare habitos'*); instead of codifying traditional forms of behaviour, it glorifies the new. Thanks to fashion, our relationship with identity is moveable, ironic and uncertain, carried by a rhythm of change that drives everyone to rethink or reject the old in favour of new elements and forms.

If our clothing has served in making our identity an object of continual construction, this is because it is more sensitive to the subtlest psychological differences. The distinction that modern clothing expresses has nothing to do with the simple economic and social distance that separates classes. Dress code became fashion when it stopped having to signify the simple distinction of class and rank or had to affirm the difference of gender or that even more subtle difference of personality or inner tendency to class or gender. It was no longer an expression of the difference of economic means but the use that each person made of the same resources.

On the other hand, an identity that can be manipulated becomes physically inseparable from all other artefacts. That is why the modern individual is built primarily through the things that he or she uses personally or is surrounded by. Artefacts, meanwhile, and especially those given the task of contributing to the construction of identity, will be defined less and less by a function or a value, whether aesthetic or economic, and instead will acquire a moral efficacy. Things must assist the transformation of the person that carries them; they are intensifiers of personality. As an objectified and reified identity – a sort of *prêt-à-porter* self – every item of clothing makes it possible to give an objective and public – and no longer a purely psychological – character to personality and identity (and for this very reason renders it communicable): it becomes the attribute of objects and the expression of a consciousness. It also makes it possible to create a distance, as Simmel writes, 'through which the exaggerated subjectivity of modernity finds a counterweight and is hidden'.

Clothing is the space in which the quality of an object can embody the feelings and attitudes of an individual and, at the same time, it is the space for translation and fusion between the objective and the subjective sphere. And it is for this reason alone that it enables us to complete our personality and our 'I'. Each feeling, each emotion, each psychological attitude is not a purely mental fact, but must become a physiology of the material world: consciousness exists in clothing, it's a carnival of colours, shapes and sizes. Morality is not really a human faculty, but a power that man can acquire only through things. Talking about the self no longer means talking about actions, attitudes, personalities or wishes, but means above all talking about objects that we put on us – about their form, their quality, or more precisely about their power over our personality and those of others.

Wearing an item of clothing is an exercise of the gestural and moral equivalence between the self and things: clothes represent the self as existing in the things we use, produce, imagine, purchase and consume. The self no longer consists in the extent to which it allows us to distinguish ourselves from the things we produce and use, but in the focus of indistinction between subject and world, between consciousness and material universe. A woollen tie seems to embody my character more than my face or my hands. The shoes I wear now seem a more genuine expression of my desire for freedom than my lungs and my hair. Fashion is possible once we discover that we can inhabit the world just as we inhabit our body; we can establish with portions of this world a form of cohabitation that is more than anatomical. This compels us to redraw the entire psychosomatic geography of the cosmos: souls are artefacts, mobile and inorganic bodies that we use and constantly penetrate and abandon. Our soul is a golem, a portion of non-innervated body with no sense organs, no mouth, that is not able to grow or to talk; we do not hear it, we are not brought up with it and yet for an instant we are in that mass of wool, leather, cotton or polyester.

The outrage of clothing is precisely this: in showing that the psyche is not a subtle fluid but an inorganic body, that it does not depend on its brain and senses and is more intense and more apparent in a skirt and jacket or a pair of trousers than in the curve of its nose or the colour of its hair. A soul is not the force that allows us to distinguish ourselves from all other non-living bodies, that allows us to resume that same portion of matter that we have inhabited for decades and to rise again after death; it is the force that allows us to penetrate any molecule and to live also in a body with which we have no organic and genealogical relationship. It is not the energy that separates humanity from all other living forms, but instead what enables any living entity to merge with all that which is not able to live. It is not the frontier that separates us from the world, but the key that allows us to enter any of its places. The purpose of clothes – like souls – is not to separate but to mix peoples, cultures, times and sentiments. Clothes are the means by which identities are contaminated and circulated. As a result of the clothes that inhabit us, we will always have on us the soul of someone else and, vice versa, we will always be the spectres that visit bodies about which we know nothing.

An item of clothing changes the psychic landscape in us and outside us: here too it is a variation of the home. Space ceases to be purely public at the point where clothing makes its appearance: it's as if, having yielded to one individual will, it takes colours, shapes and meanings that are no longer open to all but defined by one personality.

An item of clothing – whether it's a spacesuit or a tent that can follow us anywhere and has no need to tie itself to one specific territory or space – can transform any place and can transform itself virtually into a home: through fashion we are simply giving a different form to our domesticity. Our apartments, in any event, are the psychic force embodied in every item of clothing raised to the nth power. Clothes and homes both supplement the 'I': we need them to help us build and give form to our psychic life. We build homes and make clothes not to protect the body, but because the body is not enough for the soul. The 'I' is always worldly; it lives outside our body. We can never say 'I' without relying on the world.

If every item of clothing is the paradigm of the place in which we live, we ought to learn to consider the home in the same way as we consider clothes. In this way we would free ourselves from the idea that a home ought to reflect our nature once and for all; we are accustomed to making it into a kind of uniform, a garment we don't want to remove, and which we claim should resemble our skin. It's as though, so far as homes go, we were still in the age of the sumptuary laws, when clothing had to express membership of a particular class and display a certain form of opulence. Thinking about homes as a collective and more heightened form of clothing would allow us to consider them as a psychic rather than a spatial matter. And it would free us from the patrimonial and patriarchal logic by which they become an asset to be passed on through inheritance. We ought to learn to abhor the idea of living in a single home, and ought to change home in the same way that we change clothes, each entering the homes of others in the same way that we dress in other people's clothes. In the end, the home of the future ought to resemble a sort of extension and radicalization of the logic embodied in Airbnb. We ought to change home every season, just as we need to do with our clothing.

6

TWINS

For years, it was a photograph that gave me a clearer idea of home. A black and white picture, yellowed by time. It shows two little boys toddling about in a meadow. They must be around a year old since their walking is still unsteady. One, dressed in jeans and black and white striped T-shirt, is right in the middle of the picture: he is looking at the camera with an air of defiance, arms open, as if to run more easily towards the viewer. The other, dressed in dungarees, is a few yards behind: he seems to be trying to reach the first, as quickly as he can, so much so that he's lost his balance and is about to fall. There's a woman sitting in the background, some distance behind the two children. She seems to be saying something, talking to someone else who is mostly out of view. I've no idea where the photo was taken. It was around the house when I was a child. And, together with others, it was the

subject of a special quest during those surreal evenings (that now form part of my daily archaeology)
spent looking at family pictures, when we used to
leaf through photo albums or view slides of travels
and past times.

My parents, most of all my mother, custodian of
pictures and household memories, often picked it
up to show us, and played a kind of backward version of the 'Guess Who?' game. The two children
were in fact my twin brother Matteo and me. If the
quest were necessary, it was because everyone
would always mix us up, in real life and in photos
too. For years, like nearly all twins, I was accustomed to answering to my brother's name or to my
own without regard. Depending on the circumstances and the people concerned, I was Emanuele
(the real one), or the 'Emanuele' who had been
confused with Matteo, or the 'Matteo' who had
been taken for Emanuele. Like almost all twins,
other people thought my brother and I were perfectly interchangeable. And maybe not just other
people.

While we had no difficulty (at least seemingly) in
knowing who was in fact who, when it came to pictures our certainty proved far less solid. As for me,

at least, I could never identify myself in childhood photos. The quest to which our mother had accustomed us therefore had a therapeutic purpose: it restored order and identity to the mind and rooted this order in a strict visual and morphological lineage. Even today, some of her comments during this strange quest echo in my mind: 'You're the one with the oval face,' she would repeat, 'while your brother has the flat nose.'

Despite the number of evenings spent driving it into us, this rather shaky prosopography, built using our childhood photos, was never effective. Each time, we had to go back to the beginning, had to involve ourselves once more in this drawing-room Lombrosian physiognomic explanation: we had to strive once again to distinguish between one face and the other, to recognize ourselves in one body rather than another, to fix our memory to clear and distinct recollections. It was rather like a ritual celebration of the impossibility of what Lacan called 'the mirror stage'. According to Lacan, only when children manage to recognize their own image in a mirror and identify themselves with it under the authority of their parent's gaze can they finally free themselves from 'motor impotence and nursling dependence', to strengthen their self through the construction of an ideal 'I'. This ideal 'I' will permit the normalization of desire. In my case there was a reversal and an excessive inversion: not only was I unable to identify myself, but my mother's gaze, deep down, seemed unable to limit itself to touching my image alone, as if it were compelled to pass from one figure to the other, and each time to wipe away the boundaries that separated me from all other bodies.

Despite being so repetitive, this quest brought me much amusement, and it was precisely this repeated and hopeless failure that gave me pleasure. I loved finding myself up against the momentary experience of not knowing who I was. I liked being confused with the other. I liked above all hiding behind, or rather, inside the identity of the other.

There was something fleeting, something profoundly intoxicating about this quest, but it was only later, much later, that I began to understand. I was still an adolescent when I left my parents' home to further my education, and left Italy a few years later. The photograph and the curious spiritual quest that lay behind it were forgotten about for some considerable time, until a couple of years ago, when I took my daughter to visit my parents. She was about the same age that my brother and I were in the photo. Once through the front door, we climbed the staircase, slowly, step by step. The walls of the stairwell were literally covered, as they had always been, with pictures from the past – photos of my parents as children, of me, my brother and my sister. When my daughter saw all those children, she started asking who the figures were. It was then, for the first time in many years, that I saw the framed photo at the top of the stairs, lost in a photographic mosaic that had transformed this part of the house into a kind of secular votive chapel. I must have passed it dozens of times in the previous few years without ever noticing it. It was my daughter who picked it out, as if Lacan's mirror phase had been inverted: if, in this last stage, the adult enables the child to confirm their identity by declaring that the image is truly theirs, then my daughter brought me back to this strange impossibility of confirming which body in the picture was mine.

This new encounter was like a madeleine, both amusing and disturbing. On the one hand I was truly amazed and amused to see how, once again, I found it impossible to recognize my own face – mine and only mine – to rediscover my past – the past that was exclusively mine – and to give a clear aspect to my childhood. In front of this evidence that was so easy to interpret, I was faced once again with the impossibility of telling my daughter where I was, in which of those two children's bodies I'd walked. On the other hand, the situation was disturbing, very disturbing, because in the meantime my brother had died. To repeat this quest, facing once again the impossibility of visually dividing our faces and our fates, meant facing the impossibility of grief, or my inability to separate his death from my life. Seeing that picture again was like experiencing a double trauma, since the difficulty or the impossibility of grief had not re-emerged merely in the form of an emotion but had been presented in the form of a mirror image before my eyes. As if the unconscious that jumbles everything was no longer in the lower chamber of my mind but was there in front of me, in front of every other human being, in broad daylight, too visible, blinding, almost fatal.

It was only then that I realized how much that picture had transformed the strange cognitive disorder that prevented me from identifying myself in the most ordinary act of self-awareness: it had become my *cogito*, the way to say 'I am', in an endless spiritual quest, almost as if it were a destiny. And above all, it had become the form of my relationship with the world.

'Home' in a certain sense was for me the name for the desperate and often forlorn attempt to extend, to repeat, and above all to radicalize the sentiment, the posture, the way of being that this picture had imposed on me since early childhood. For a long time, I imagined that this meant a particular taste for the secret. And yet nothing in this experience was hidden, nothing was invisible. On the contrary, it was all there, in the photo, visible and clear. Neither of the two could recognize their own face, neither could combine knowledge and realization. Or better still, they both knew too much. Because the problem was not one of knowing who I was, but of finding myself in the situation of suddenly having two possible self-awarenesses, two possible faces, and of not being able to choose between them. It was not the experience of being unable to say 'I', but the experience of being able to say it at least twice – something much stranger and more difficult to describe. I was dealing not with the disappearance of my childhood memory, but with its virtual duplication. I was not compelled to do without my body, I did not see or feel my soul living without a body and without organs: on the contrary, I found it impossible to assign my soul to one single body or give my body to a single soul. Home, for me, has always been the name for the intoxication that this gulf, ontological as well as moral, has stirred in me since my childhood.

Intoxication: this picture contains within it a surfeit of possibilities and seems to render them all equally legitimate, all equally imprecise and all equally unstable. At any moment someone else, the Other One or Other Ones, my brother or other twins, might arrive and pretend to be what I think I am – in the photo as well as in reality. At any moment someone else might pretend to be me, and to be me differently from me. At any moment, above all (and this is the most difficult part of being a twin), I can tell myself that the Other One embodies my being but does it much better than me.

That picture expresses something that has often been described and which the experience of twin-ship brings to daily and intimate apparency. It is not a question of being forced to confide in the other, as is often mentioned with all the good intentions in the world but with a hint of sanctimonious and tiresome moralism. Nor is it an invitation to respect the other or to love your neighbour as yourself. It's the proof that identity, or rather the correspondence between the self and the other, is an ontological fact and not a moral duty. It's the proof that this identity between me and the other is much more disturbing, much more surprising than I had imagined. In front of this photo, relating to myself means always being unable to distinguish myself from the other, and recognizing myself entirely in the features of my brother's face. This excess of faces and identities is disturbing because it is in fact infinite and has forced me to rewrite a surreal and farcical version of the Cartesian *cogito*.

Like Alice in front of the looking glass, I have always considered this picture to be proof of the perfect convertibility between inside and outside: in me, in the depths of my intimacy, I always discover the world, an external reality, of which my brother was only one piece, a fragment modelled by a strange game of fate to my image and likeness. Or maybe I, myself, was modelled on the image and likeness of my brother, identical and therefore indistinguishable from the vast world outside, from all that was happening between my skin and the horizon. Here too the problem is not lack, but excess of recognition and self-awareness: there's a 'self' inside me and outside me, and it's not possible to recognize the line that transforms introspection into perception, organ into instrument, self into world, and vice versa.

The gulf is therefore not just cognitive or moral: it's like confronting a cosmic error. It's not just a conundrum in the mechanism of recognition. What is more frightening, and intoxicating, is the realization that the life inside me – in the most intimate part of my being (my heart, brain and DNA), the life that has never stopped generating me – is exactly the same as that in someone else. The contemplation of this other life which is at the same time and with equal right elsewhere and within me, which can exist inside me and outside me, was my original experience of the home. My body and that of my brother express exactly the same life – an indeterminate life, protean and omnivorous, capable of going elsewhere, of becoming anything else, of transforming itself into anything else.

A home is a space where life can circulate freely between bodies: it offers a sort of magic that allows people and objects to become twins, at least for a moment. Home, at least for me, was the name for the sorcery of twinship: the forms generated by this unconscious desire to identify myself with something else, and by the impossibility of ever being sure whether what I was looking at was a twin whose likeness had been temporarily lost – a caterpillar which, on becoming a butterfly, had lost its resemblance to me but secretly kept the same life that existed in me. As if the real, human twin were constantly in other possible or virtual twins. As if the whole world were simply the enormous palette of a common twinship, no longer biological (or cosmic) but terrestrial, concrete, existential; not just this girlfriend, this woman, this man, but also the earth, water, the chicken I ate for lunch, the computer on which I am writing this book, my telephone, money, the air we breathe. They are aniconic, cosmic, metaphorical twins that give expression to my own life and my own breath.

Each time that twinship becomes our home, it

is no longer a single fate that connects certain beings, excluding others. It is the fabric of the world and of society. Twinship is not the relationship that bound me to my brother: it's the form of relationship that every being has with him or herself and with the world. It's not a question of appearance, of sharing a form, but of structure and of flesh: the whole world shares the same life, and differences of form are only the scars of the transformations that have accumulated since the original birth of all living beings. We cosmic twins share the same life, but each person sets it on a different course, gives it a particular inflection.

I have fought hard against this tendency to identify myself with any other thing and have viewed it as a pathology, a serious pathology. In a certain sense it is. It is most of all a moral pathology. Twins are ruled by a social and emotional curse: that of having to taste the forbidden fruit of love, of absolute intimacy with another, but without a love story, with no crude and arduous sequence of sublime and disastrous encounters, of pleasures and torments, of quarrels and reconciliations. It is the paradoxical experience of being able to say 'Amen' without needing to recite together the sad rosary of

promises and betrayals, expectations and mono-
logues, oversights and surprises. Intimacy with a
twin is, literally, prehistoric. It exists prior to every
form of experience, and is immemorial, incomprehensible and above all unjustifiable even to those
who live it. My brother and I could go for months
without seeing or talking to each other, yet it took
only a second to feel that the soul of the other
was an extension of our own. It has been the
greatest difficulty of my life to accept that that
same intimacy was a gift, which arrives sometimes
at the end of a journey of sharing. It is never its
precondition.

It was even more difficult to realize that sexual
love had to be different. In my dealings with Eros, I
found myself always inside the myth of androgyny,
but multiplied and expanded out of proportion: as
if half of myself was everywhere, in every woman
and man, in every object, in every occurrence. It is
probably for this reason that I fall in love with
everyone and everything. Not in the sense of superficial enthusiasm: I always have the feeling of being
with a duplicate of myself – everywhere.

On an ontological level, the risk is that of con-
fusing the doctrine of world – cosmogony – with

the extension of self, a delusion of omnipotence. And yet, to recognize a potential twin in every object is the exact opposite of the wish to take over or dominate. It does not mean projecting our personality onto him or her but, on the contrary, forcing ourselves to regard each object or each body as a source of self-understanding. In a world of 'universal twinship', every act of self-understanding must pass through an understanding of the other, and understanding the world comes through understanding oneself. On the other hand, if everything is a twin, everything has the same rights and the same secrets as our so-called unconscious. Recognizing that there's a cosmic twinship that passes through everything, declaring that we are all twins who have lost or refashioned their likeness, does not simply mean that the world is a double. There is no longer just one duplicate of us in the world, everything is duplicating something else. Acknowledging cosmic twinship means declaring that there are in me duplicates of others, identical characteristics I had never suspected, which the encounter with others reveals and revives.

Because of this picture, I cannot rid myself of the idea that, beyond every pathology, beyond every

grief, twinship is not a casual biographical circum-
stance reserved to a few human beings. It is the
most intense form of something deeper and vaster,
the concentration of the relationship that unites all
women and men, all species, all beings.

It is not a purely genealogical bond. On the contrary, it is always a breakdown, a dysfunction of
genealogy, the horizontal and infinite extension of
kinship to the detriment of the verticality of the
trees that genealogy so loves. It was not our mother
or our father who transformed me and my brother
into twins. Our mother indeed suffered for our
being twins; especially in the literal sense, because
she was forced to spend months in bed, being eaten
alive by two small humanoid fishes who were party-
ing inside her womb. But principally in the
metaphysical sense: it is not the parent that makes
twins, it is the life force itself and its capacity to
pass anywhere, to penetrate and give life to any
body, to transform itself into any material and any
object in the world. This same life that crafts our
flesh and makes us live side by side, in a continual
exchange of liquids, padded noises, kicking, space
and time in the mother's womb and out of it. This
exchange which ensures that one person becomes

the other, and vice versa, is a movement much more present, incessant and repeated than we imagine. It's the breath of our universe, the physiology of our world.

We produce twins by breathing, inspiring all that we have in front of us and transforming it into the blood of our blood, constantly hybridizing with all that is outside us. Twinship is not the result of sharing the same mother and the same father, but an extra-genealogical and extra-ontological consanguinity. It's the art of being intoxicated by all things. We produce it by speaking, for the words we utter are always our twins. Twinship is a viral contagion much more than a genetic structure. We generate it by eating, transforming the flesh of others into our flesh, and turning our flesh into the reincarnation of another life. It is less a morphological resemblance than a repetition, a reincarnation of each of the other bodies.

Like a cosmic twin with thousands of doubles, we all concentrate in our body the echoes of billions of different individuals, species and times. Like cosmic twins, we re-echo the whole history of the world in our every action. We can inhabit it simply because each time we say 'I am' we make every 'I am' of our twins re-echo in the universe, because thanks to this cosmic twinship our consciousness corresponds virtually with the cosmos.

A home is simply the consciousness of this twinship, of this love for twins spread across the planet. They are always many more than two.

7

WHITE POWDER

No home is ever finished. We never stop building it. Not only modifying the geometry of its rooms, changing the catalogue of things allowed inside, but also dressing it up, associating other lives with our daily intimacy, making love, sleeping. But for me, the most radical experience in homemaking is writing. It doesn't matter where I am. Whether in Berlin, Frankfurt, New York, Paris, Florence or Barcelona, the scene is set in just the same way. The shutters are closed, the blinds are lowered. For days, sunlight is banished from the house. My circadian rhythm adapts. Time stops dividing itself according to the movements of the sun and lengthens into a corridor that becomes a perennial northern winter, into a long night of spectres and visions. Hours pass in the mysterious choreography of my hands.

My fingers in these moments form strange

strokes that seem like scribbles on a smooth white surface. They draw pothooks and downstrokes, for no apparent reason, and measure the relationship between stems and serifs. In short, they trace out letters on a page. It seems a harmless activity. Yet the effect of these aniconic inscriptions on the mind can be compared to that of a nuclear bomb on human bodies: apart from the immediate violence of the explosion, there's an invisible, evasive, irreparable influence that stretches for centuries.

Writing demonstrates this strange radioactivity of the mind: a capacity to occupy the simplest, poorest, least 'animated' material – an idea becomes an ink mark on a cellulose surface – and then, from this minute existence, to exercise a much greater, more powerful, lasting influence than it did when it occupied the brain of one individual. Writing is not a substitute for speech, as has often been suggested. It probably has an accidental connection with words and language.

We are accustomed to producing something ordinary, commonplace and extremely innocuous with writing. And yet it is one of the most potent psychotropic substances that exist. The effect these irregular strokes have on those using them is to create visions – in the widest sense of the word, which includes all the senses and reason: we begin seeing, hearing, tasting, thinking about beings that are absent and have no substantial connection with the series of marks we have in front of us. There's nothing documentary. Nothing photographic. Nothing realistic. Even when we really want to say what we've seen. Any kind of reading, from this point of view, can be compared to taking LSD or ayahuasca. Words are white powder, or some unpleasant tasting drink. But sip by sip, something appears before us, something that has nothing to do with our body or with the world around us – with one crucial difference: thanks to this substance we can control the vision, personally induce it and, above all, reproduce it whenever we wish.

Those who write undergo the opposite process to that which occurs among those taking psychedelic drugs: in the latter case, a material substance generates a vision, while in the former, a vision leads the person who is writing to secrete an anomalous psychotropic substance (language is basically just this, psychedelia within anyone's reach) that makes it possible to invoke and replicate countless times that vision which the writer has experienced.

This is also why its power is so enduring, and why it is so widely used. We need these visions. Our body is nourished by the life that animates everything around us. That is why we are obliged to eat: we stay alive only by including and metabolizing life outside our anatomy. That is why we have sensory organs: they allow life – light, sound and noise, hardness, tastes, sweetness in its most varied forms – to pass through us. There are parts of life, however, that cannot be assimilated through food, nor by using our sensory organs.

Writing gives us another way of continuing what we do by eating and perceiving the world: to experience the whole of life around us and let it pass through us. It produces an intimacy between all things and all living beings that goes back before the order of proximity constructed by birth, by eating and by perception. It produces a spiritual continuity where there is no direct continuity of any other kind. All beings constantly invent ways of penetrating each other, of living the life of the Other, of becoming the Other. And the life of each one of them can thus pass from one body to the other, from individual to individual, from species to species, from place to place, from one time to another. Writing, and the vision to which it grants access, are at the same time the origin, the evidence and the record of this continuity. There's nothing intellectual about it. It's an injection of life's pure, chemical, responsive, visionary substance: life concentrated in drops of ink whose powers are inexhaustible, irrepressible. All writing is a trick that life has invented to penetrate us, to change us for ever, before slipping away elsewhere. All writing frees life from ever belonging to any one person; it allows it to remain an eternal wanderer.

We need home for the same reason that we need writing. Ordinary experience is never sufficient: it's not enough to perceive the world as it is, it's not enough to be a part of it by fixing our silhouette upon its surface. Starting off from its reality and ours, we need to create a vision, a mixture of colours, sounds, aromas and emotions. At the same time, we cannot inhabit the world in its purity by searching for the place that occupies the least space. Inhabiting the world means transforming its structure, it means becoming the writing of the planet itself.

An ancient illusion drives us to imagine a home as part of the world, just like all the other things around it. Nothing inside it seems especially different from what is found elsewhere: stone, steel, glass, timber and other chemical elements that make up the world seem to be the same as the constituents of the commonplace objects that populate it and, above all, every home is inhabited by people who can live elsewhere. Fuelled also by a deep sense of urban and ecological guilt, we do all we can to emphasize the continuity of our home with the environment in which it stands. And yet, if this really were so, if a home was composed of the same substances as the world, if there really were the same things inside as there are outside, if we were always to find the same quality of time, if the life held within its walls was identical to what lay beyond them, then we wouldn't need homes.

The shape of the home is of little importance – as are its style, size or fabric. It matters little whether it's a tent, a mountain hut, or a seventeenth-century palace. It matters little what purpose or reason we have for building it – as shelter from bad weather, to hold our possessions or for intimate moments with those we love. We make homes to break every form of continuity with reality, not just physical, climatic, biological or ecological, but above all psychic and spiritual. It's not just a matter of interruption. A home is above all the arbitrary insertion, inclusion, addition of a different, other, supernumerary space and time.

Windows and *trompe l'œils*, gardens and solid foundations, may modify but won't overturn the fact that being at home means creating a different and personal climate against the weather outside: another light, a different humidity, but also another love, other temperaments, other timescales, unfolding at a pace that differs from that of the city. Being at home always means choosing from a catalogue of acts opposed to those that our body performs beneath the sun. It's not a question of modesty. We confuse difference and isolation; we transform a cosmic autonomy into a petit-bourgeois desire to stand out socially and psychologically. This alterity cannot even be reduced to the contrast between an inside and an outside. Likenesses must not deceive us. Every home is a cave that places on the planet square metres and minutes that it will never own. It presupposes the opening of a gap of inconsistency with all that surrounds it, and which breaks every flow and every ecosystem, introduces an alien element which even as it feeds on what surrounds it does not share its flesh.

Every home is an operation of cosmic surgery that produces extraterritorial pockets on a planetary scale. An extraterrestrial invasion. A home is a volcano that spews onto the planet an alternative time and space, an unworldly reality. Alien space. Instead of taking this space from the centre of the Earth, each home takes it from an indeterminate elsewhere. The home is the real 'outside', seen from the planet. As we write, we introduce elements into the experience that cannot be deduced or predicted from the surrounding context nor from our actual experience. Similarly, as we live, we introduce something into a geographical and ecological context that cannot be predicted or deduced from the environment. Just as honey is secreted in a hive, likewise every house secretes and pours out a different experience. It's a volcano in reverse, a volcano that spews sky onto earth: a celestial volcano that throws onto the Earth a celestial lava; a space and time that has nothing to do with what surrounds it.

On the other hand, walking into a house – it doesn't matter how rich or poor – is always a voyage into time and into space. An intergalactic journey that takes us into another atmosphere, another ecosystem, towards another population, another time. A black hole, an unfathomable mystery. That is why it is ludicrous to imagine that home can describe a form of autochthony. Once we have entered someone's house, we become planetary migrants, tourists in other people's psychedelia.

The journey into the soul of the person who lives there carries you far from the surrounding city. It is not the identification of a home with a place that makes it what it is. Instead, it is all homes together, by emanation and echo, that define the identity of a place.

There is something profoundly anti-spatial in our homes. And that is why every home is so dangerous for the city, for nature, for the Earth. It is an anti-geographical force, a current of world geographical unrealism. It is not a phantasmagoria that projects a different image of reality onto stones, as the city does: the home has to construct another world.

All of this could be summarized by saying that the underlying operation in every home is the metamorphosis of space into place. Thanks to the home, something different is established through the harmonious expansion of matter, in just the same way that, thanks to the word, an alien reality exists in a tiny fragment of matter (whether voice or page) that has nothing to do with the word. Home is the arbitrary insistence of an elsewhere, a journey on the spot: it is autonomous, just as the signified is arbitrary and autonomous in relation to the signifier. It is a form of writing, but cosmic, made with the planet's skin, with its flesh, its bones, its hair. Every time we build homes – we, and every other living creature – one portion of the Earth becomes psychedelic matter. Honey.

8

SOCIAL MEDIA

Any artefact is an extension of the will to set up home, of the desire to transform the world in order to live in it. Every time we manipulate matter, we are trying to tame the planet, to turn it into our home and, vice versa, to let ourselves be tamed by it. In no other artefact is this desire for home so evident as in social media. Since the 1950s the home has been invaded by new 'electrical appliances' – fridges, washing machines, televisions, computers – each made to radically transform our domestic experience, to invest it with a new form of energy. Maybe that is why the home has become the design model for digital space.

We hardly notice it, yet Facebook or Instagram are extensions or projections of domestic space. They are literally distorted utopian images of a new way of conceiving domestic sociality. As homes, of course, they are paradoxical. Like clothing, they follow us everywhere, but we don't need to hold these homes tight around our skin. To get into them, all we need do is open our laptop or unlock our mobile phone and tap in a few characters. It's as though we have transformed our old family photo album into a real, habitable space. But unlike the family album, this immense 'Book of Faces' doesn't look to the past but to the present. And while those albums portrayed a family that already existed, through this strange audiovisual bible we can construct a new non-genealogical family, choosing the faces with whom to share our intimate moments, starting from a catalogue that strives to include every human being.

It's a strange form of portable paradise where each person chooses their own Adam or Eve. Cities and states don't exist in this world. This new planetary home is an immense royal court where everyone is, at the same time, queen or king and courtier. The community doesn't appear with monarchs or courtiers fixed to one specific place. The geography is no longer real. There are no French, Italians, Japanese or Brazilians.

Genealogical ties are irrelevant. The house of faces recognizes only one social bond: friendship.

This gives no guarantee at all of peace and harmony: the anonymity and secrecy that every city offers and assures is impossible among friends. Everyone knows each other and above all – as in every royal court – everyone watches and judges everyone else. To be a good courtier requires great effort – the endless capacity to pretend to be what you are not without revealing too much about what you want to be. It's what, in Renaissance times, was called *sprezzatura*.

The house of friends that we have created in digital space seems to prefigure a world that doesn't yet exist. Facebook, Instagram or WhatsApp represent the yearning for a strange brand of virtual monastic existence, the possibility of living in close vocal and visual contact with hundreds or thousands of people, bypassing cities but, most of all, totally disregarding the walls that define the geometry of our homes. Through these new 'domestic appliances', the home – the building that allowed us to be close to objects and people – looks more like Charles Fourier's phalansteries than the bourgeois imagination that organizes our cities. Thanks to these, we seem to be living in two domestic spaces, one nesting inside the other, which yet seem to come from two different epochs, one projected towards the future, while the other is intent on closing the past inside a cement shell.

It's as though, through the contrasting forms and ways in which we exist in one space and the other, these new digital homes were revealing how our homes of stone and steel were strange time machines, enormous incubators that could transport us each night to a distant epoch. Walking in through the front door of our home means turning back the clock, going back in time, being catapulted back into the nineteenth century. The vast, friendly, international space of the court of faces is transformed like Cinderella's coach into the stone and steel prisons of our solitude. In comparison to these homes that we yearn for and inhabit through digital prostheses, our own homes, our apartments, seem like obsolete machines – large boxes built to distil our life for distinct purposes.

Above all, in these spaces we are forced to live first and foremost according to the social rules and ways of the past, wavering usually between the extremes of monastic solitude and the nuclear family (father-mother-child). Community and the sharing of every intimate moment with friends throughout the world, which is the spatial form of the great court of faces, become a simple dream. Our apartments, in comparison, seem like mental devices for distancing, which push aside all human forms that don't belong to our genealogical families. During the months of the great global pandemic, I often wondered what our lives would have been like if the virus had not made our cities inaccessible but our homes. What would have happened if we had all been forced to live rough and homeless, with no roofs over our heads? I often wondered if, in that case, we would have let ourselves follow the line of our friendships and affections, rethinking our choice of those we live with. Are we capable of imagining and constructing domestic realities modelled on relationships different from those of family or of solitude?

The great court of faces is just one of the thousand corridors that recent technology has opened up between habitations, bypassing the city. To organize physical stones and homes in the same way that we organize these corridors will depend on our ability to understand the radical transformation in the nature and scope of the technology and machinery around us. We can hardly manage to say it, and yet, from a technology whose scope was the performance of physical tasks, we have moved to machines whose task is the extension, the multiplication and the explosion of human psychism. This evolution has been badly interpreted as a result of the dominance of the metaphor and the cognitive or cybernetic vocabulary which have led us to talk only about the brain, intelligence and thought. We are used to making crude distinctions: we separate mind and intelligence and think the brain is where intelligence lies. For this reason alone, we imagine that computers and mobile telephones are extensions of our brain and not an amplification of our psychic life.

Yet what has happened over the past hundred years is more than clear. The traditional machine is based on an imitation of the physical organism: according to Ernst Kapp, every machine is the projection of an anatomical organ outside the human body. New machines, on the other hand, are based on an imitation of the life of the psyche, and it doesn't matter whether that relates to intelligence, calculation, imagination or feeling, etc. This is exemplified by photography, the cinema and computers, but above all by mobile phones. They project the psyche outside human consciousness and anatomy. And while traditional machines made it possible for human bodies themselves to exert a subjective force externally and direct it towards an objective, the new machines make the soul exist outside us, they turn the life of the psyche into a feature that can exist not only in the human anatomy but in any object, and which can come alive at any moment.

The development of these new technologies has responded to a profound anthropological, moral and political need: the invention of computers, mobile phones and the technologies that make them a collective platform for generating and sharing intimacy is not a coincidental result of a few chance discoveries, but a conscious construction that has emerged out of a *Kunstwollen*, a specific artistic and anthropological will. All these machines are in fact symbolic forms that respond to moral requirements – for the construction of the individual.

It was Schiller who showed that subjectivity cannot be grasped either as a bare cognitive fact or as an arbitrary act of will: it exists in an intermediate sphere – that of art and play – where knowledge and will, science and morality merge together. It is

PHILOSOPHY OF THE HOME

in pursuit of this intuition that art became not only the space for the construction of decorative beauty (or of the definition of a non-normative sharing, as it was in Kant), but also the preferred workshop for the invention of the individual.

For almost a century we have required literature and the pictorial and plastic arts to invent and bring visibility to the structure of our 'I': novels and art-works have enabled us to understand the form that the lives of our minds and our feelings have assumed. Throughout the twentieth century the 'I' was the place and the means through which each of us could experience as an epiphany (in other words, in an instantaneous, uncontrollable and unpro-grammed way) our own belonging to a psychic flow older than our own conscious memories and broader than our own personality. James Joyce's *Ulysses*, Virginia Woolf's *Mrs Dalloway*, Marcel Proust's *In Search of Lost Time*, and Jackson Pollock's action painting allowed the 'I' to be structured in this way.

For less than two decades, the task which had been assigned for centuries to the arts, that of fash-ioning our 'I', has been taken over by other symbolic, more hybrid and unreliable forms, but ones that are also more universal and radical than those that the art system had been able to classify. These forms are social media: a sort of collective open-ended novel in which everyone is, at the same time, author, character and interpreter of how their own life is interwoven with that of others. It's an augmented and extended form of literature – augmented because the fractured manner in which literature has divided characters from authors and spectators has been cancelled out. That is why reality and fiction no longer stand in conflict.

A few years ago, the Argentinean critic Josefina Ludmer described the current state of literature, noting that fiction was no longer 'a genre or a specific phenomenon, but instead covered reality until it merged with it'. The problem is not just that 'fiction merges with reality', but that 'the new regime changes the constitution of fiction and the very notion of literature', because 'literature absorbs the mimesis of the past to fabricate the present and reality'. Reality itself is fabricated literarily, artistically. This is the constitution that Ludmer calls 'post-autonomous literature': that for which, rather than producing art – in other words a sphere of reality detached from normal custom and life – it becomes a 'factory of reality'. The new media have enabled literature – no longer limited to the written word – to transform itself in this space: they are no longer limited, elitist practices but a collective act of existence, forms of homemaking that no longer follow any past model.

In them, personal and emotional realities have to be simulated and imagined in order to be experienced. That is why there is no distinction between author and character: for it is only through becoming a fictional character that one acquires the status of author, and not vice versa. And being an author now means having access to one's own exclusive reality through a literary fiction. It's an augmented form of literature because the medium on which it is exercised is not purely verbal but consists of a series of supports that seek to reproduce the experience as far as possible. It is extended because it involves a truly remarkable number of users in comparison to traditional arts. In the end, it accomplishes the task that historic avant-garde movements had set for art – of corresponding with life. For this very reason, new artistic practices have taken the home as their blueprint, have overrun and contaminated the domestic space, and have transformed its interior. They have become our new homes. They are places through which we make the social and human world habitable; the visual and literary device that allows us to be at home anywhere.

But Facebook or Instagram, however, embody a paradox. Through these platforms, experience is structured as something that must be interpreted, staged, and must become fiction in order to be more real than it is. On the other hand, it is fiction that changes in nature and purpose: it no longer serves to lead the imagination elsewhere, to unknown or unfamiliar worlds or different lives. Instead, it must allow the person who is creating it to coincide as much as possible with his or her own life. Life becomes an auto-fiction whose purpose is to allow the subject to become what he or she is. Each person is the custodian of this paradox: on the one hand, they are the writer of a real-life drama, whose theatre corresponds with the world we see in front of us, while, on the other hand, they are the interpreter of their own existence, of a life written and composed also by others.

If life becomes the object of an aesthetic construction, all the ingredients that make up our experience can be manipulated through its simple image. There's no longer any difference between an object and its representation. That is why the writing of this new literature must occupy all media, it must blur them together in the same way that everything in the world blurs together its own visual, tactile, olfactory and rational identities. And there's not even a spatial separation: to be conscious of something it's not necessary to separate its image from the world, but to turn consciousness out into the world. We have to carry our consciousness into the world and not the world into our consciousness. The metaphor of consciousness is no longer the camera obscura: consciousness is out in the open. It is image inside image. Experience always occurs outside us, because, thanks to these new homes, psyche and world are the same thing. The life of our psyche no longer takes place exclusively inside our body, but also and especially outside it. It's as if we had become aware that experience could live outside us, could reverberate around us, not just through writing or cinema.

Through these machines that imitate the life of the soul, we are building together a kind of new 'soul of the world', a collective psyche, to which each of us is subject only to the extent to which we are content or character. Consciousness is only a vehicle, something that allows an emotion, knowledge or perception to be transmitted elsewhere. Consciousness is contagious and becomes viral. Through these machines, however, we are changing above all the nature of the world. For the world itself is now, for us, becoming a psychical fact. The world no longer consists of events; it consists of a common psyche, a consciousness in which we are all immersed.

The psyche has become world and the world is a psychical fact before it is material. It is not just cognitive, but psychic and demonic, and that is why the 'I' seems to multiply in such a viral manner. This is not just narcissism. The collective psyche is no longer something transcendental and ahistorical (like Jungian 'archetypes') but a malleable entity, and therefore poetic and aesthetic; belonging to it is linked to a decision on taste and can be manipulated endlessly.

The conflict between these two experiences of domesticity ought to be ended. The future that awaits us lies in the capacity to understand this psychic transformation of the world: our individual and collective souls are now before us. Everything depends on the form we give to this collective soul-world, in which all of us are and will be its scriptwriters and characters.

Thanks to psychomorphic machines, that is machines that imitate the shape of the soul and not that of the body, we have broken down the walls and frontiers that separated not only nations and continents but also the buildings in which all human beings lived. We have created a psychic place of sharing that lies on this side of any conflict between public and private. Thanks to psychomorphic machines, the home has lost all spatial and geographic determination, has freed itself from the city, or rather it has interiorized it, and has assumed planetary dimensions. Forecasts are obviously simplistic and often absurd. But what has become possible can no longer be ignored. This is now perhaps the moment to make geography conform with this new order, to redesign the planet like a mobile chequer board of intimacies that spreads beyond cities and beyond nations.

9

BEDROOMS AND CORRIDORS

As I remember it, I spent my childhood haunted by fear. It wasn't a constant presence, but its infrequency made its effect all the stronger. It arrived, unannounced, in the strangest and most unlikely moments. It was unpredictable, not just because it could appear in the most familiar and ordinary of situations in which it seemed impossible to shatter the confidence and happiness of a child's world. It was unpredictable especially because, when seen from a distance, it looked like any other emotion. It came out like a happy and nervous shriek of joy which I often produced, or as a milder version of the melancholy into which I liked to bury myself.

It was impossible to anticipate. It was impossible to recognize. Even when it came as the most powerful and, for me, the most obvious fear – fear of the dark. In such moments, it came in disguise, transfigured by pride and presumption, hidden by the foregone certainty that I would walk down the long corridor that separated the dining room from my bedroom without quickening my step, without panicking. The fear at such times was the most treacherous, the most farcical of emotions, ready to put on any mask to slip in anywhere. There was nothing joyous, though, about this carnival of emotions and sensations. When, at the most unlikely moment, the face-paint melted and the false appearance dropped, all became terror and anguish. And I was gripped by an immense pain, as if through the ignominy of being betrayed twice. It wasn't so much the horror and disgust at seeing the world before me turn into something disturbing and threatening. What shocked and paralysed me was the amazed bewilderment of discovering that the unrecognizable was to be found in my own 'I'. I couldn't admit that the spectre that I feared might walk through the front door, or appeared on that long corridor, was my own 'I', my own soul.

For a long while I was frightened of that corridor. It had no windows and no other things, no objects that might make it more domestic, more lived in. There was just the front door, a flimsy protection against the night-world which, for the child I was then, was an endless line of ghosts and metamorphic creatures. It was always open during the day since my mother preferred to let visitors walk in without having to ring the bell.

For a long while I was frightened of corridors, even away from home. They are barren, dark and featureless spaces: they lack the comfort of bedrooms that an adolescent can transform into a second body. They don't have the homeliness of living rooms, of words spoken in the alcove of complicity among friends, nor the richness or pleasure of food eaten in company. They are spaces of change and transformation, and yet they do not offer the possibility of becoming masters and rulers of the changes to material and spirit, as is the case in kitchens and those spaces for alchemizing what we are or would like to be – as do, for example, bathrooms. The purpose of corridors is to change place and above all to change ourselves. More than that, corridors are spaces in which the verbs we use for home – to live, to stay, to dwell – have no meaning. They are machines that force life into movement, in all its forms.

For many years I was frightened of being no

more than a long corridor, an empty space, where there was nothing truly mine, nothing intimate. I was frightened of becoming a dark place that was always windy, where no one stopped, and everyone passed through without leaving any memories, or leaving memories only with those who passed through. I was frightened of being a windowless place, with just a large, flimsy door that didn't shut properly and allowed phantoms in from the world outside, letting out the ghosts and noises of a difficult family life.

For a long while I was frightened of corridors and learned very late how to overcome these fears. I didn't need courage. Courage is useless against fear. All that is needed is desire – its stubbornness, its force, sometimes the blindness of desire. Desire alone can overcome fear. Fear is merely the force that prevents us from desiring something. That's what past thinkers taught us in their books. Spinoza wrote: 'that emotion by which a man is disposed not to want the thing he wants, and to desire that which he does not want, is called fear'.[4]

The corridor separated me from the chosen place for desire in my childhood, its special area: the bedroom. That room, as I remember it, had an aura emitted by the enormous wicker basket that contained an assortment of toys which changed over time: our model cars, our Big Jims (action figures), Lego bricks, objects sometimes in pieces but ready to be transformed into imaginary characters. They came out of that basket like a Pandora's box: to lift one out was to release an alternative cosmogony that defied our mother's futile attempt to restore all things to their daily order. My bed and my brother's bed contributed to this strange continual creation of space: they could be fixed one above the other to form a bunk bed or they could be separated. Even late at night these two beds continued as play-stations: we invented crazy radio or television shows and used to comment on the day's events. Then sleep overcame us, silence fell, and the long intermission began.

The bed is the most paradoxical object to be invented by humanity. We use it for a whole variety of purposes: we spend hours there reading, making love, staring at the ceiling, daydreaming. But most of all, a bed must accommodate, nurture and enable our lengthy mental absences. It's the theatre for daily hibernation, for our recurrent escapes. It is made for those long hours in which our body is little more than a piece of clothing left abandoned on the floor and, for everyone around us, we stop being. Even for ourselves. We absent ourselves; we leave the shared world for a few hours and exist somewhere else. Each time it is difficult to know and explain what really happens during those hours. This experience of absence, parallel to presence, we call 'dreams'. We remember them to a greater or lesser extent. We've spent centuries trying to learn from them. But in this discontinuity imposed on us each day, to disappear from the world and compel the world to disappear from us, there is something mysterious and disturbing. Karl Löwith once wrote that philosophy has never worried itself about the fact that all people spend at least a third of their days asleep. This neglect is partly due to philosophy's origins in the town and city.

We have shut our dreams up in bedrooms as we have done with gender in bathrooms. Hidden, protected from other people's gaze, the key thrown to the bottom of a river, it is the most domestic mystery of our existences. Every home, in the end, is built around this fragility of consciousness: we need homes to protect these attention losses, these moments of abstraction, and to allow them to happen. Dreaming certainly restores and regenerates us, yet it is a landslide of the 'I'. The home is both the symptom and the means of removal of this shortcoming in the life of the psyche; a garage of the soul in which we can allow ourselves, each day, for hours, to be our own *desaparecido*, to preserve a time in which, literally, we no longer know what happened, and have only the vaguest of recollections. A black hole.

Yet if the bed is important, it is less so for these prolonged and unjustifiable absences as it is for what happens after. Something snatches us from sleep, from dreams, and brings us back to the present. And instead of being aware of what is missing, thanks to a rapid and imperceptible movement we find some form of continuity between the moments when our consciousness was interrupted. 'Reawakening' is what we call this gesture of psychic surgery which has to reattach consciousness each time to a diurnal past to which we no longer have immediate access because of the dream that has intervened between the now and the then. It's not only to do with the survival of the memory or how long the recollection lasts. There's nothing automatic: an imperceptible gesture sews together shreds of unrelated presence, covers the holes and pretends that the absences never existed. The bed is an operating table of psychism and demonstrates that reorganizing the psyche is all it does, that the 'I' is a mental patchwork, the result of an operation of daily repair that makes us Frankenstein monsters in which the multiple flows of consciousness find a temporary unison before the next interruption.

If this operation in its most basic form is done in bed, reawakening in reality is everywhere: if we have consciousness, it is only because we keep stitching together the fragments of our experience, as all we are doing is reawakening – at every instant. The world is an enormous bed into which we are continually sinking and waking. Home is the form of the psychism, but it is everywhere. And consciousness is always a rag doll, a Harlequin coat to which patches are continually being added.

Rather than looking at the bed from the viewpoint of those who are awake – and continuing to pretend that psychic collapses do not exist, that the nocturnal landslides of the 'I' are an accident – we ought to learn to redefine the geography of the soul from the point of view of the bed, starting from the moment of reawakening. In order to perceive, to consider, to imagine, we need to wake up: there is no spontaneous flow, there's an imperceptible subterranean activity of suturing that constantly constructs the consciousness. Presence to the world is always a form of reawakening.

We open our eyes, and the world structures itself like consciousness in progress, which for an instant is not ours. Waking up is like installing ourselves in a consciousness already in progress: only a few seconds later do we realize that this self-awareness, this sensitive life-in-being is actually ours. It's as if we were stepping into an 'I' already present or were taking the place of an 'I' already awake, permanently awake – into our own 'I'. Reawakening is not the transition from absence of perception to presence of perception, but the intuition of a kind of autonomous, general consciousness of the world which has always been there, which we sometimes manage to appropriate and make our own. The world is already vivid, actively conscious.

For this very reason, when we awake, consciousness and memory coincide: the psychic surgery that takes place at that moment makes present, past and future come together for an instant. In reality we experience the paradox of perceiving a consciousness in progress – and of the overlapping between learning and memory of something that we have never previously perceived – much more than we imagine. Each time we listen or read we become conscious of the consciousness of others. Letting you read these lines means, literally, placing you for an instant in my self-consciousness, letting you correspond with it, and no longer knowing where my 'I' ends and where yours begins.

The word has this magic: it allows the self-consciousness of each person to become an object and, as an object, to become the self-consciousness of others. The action of every word is therefore both a reawakening and a memory: as you read, my self-consciousness written in these words is reawakened and your soul becomes the memory of the moment when I wrote these lines. Each word is the meeting point between the person known and the person knowing. That is why every apperception of language is always a reawakening.

Reawakening allows us to understand that this strange coincidence is not peculiar just to our perception of the word, but is characteristic of any act of knowledge. We are always perceiving the world's widespread, atomized, anonymous and highly personal self-consciousness. At each reawakening we touch and are touched by an infinity of past, present and future subjects. And from this point of view, every act of knowledge is knowledge gained vicariously. In each reawakening, we have a foretaste of someone else's future life and together we relive and chew over our own life or, vice versa, we allow others, when they wake, to live differently. For our lives to be a reawakening means that wakefulness is an expansion and a permanent psychic change of direction. A psychic metamorphosis of the soul of another.

Each reawakening creates a bond of continuity that wasn't there before. Continuity is different from unity; it isn't formal homogeneity, or material uniformity, it's a contagious bond of contact between different parts. The mind is always contagious, and communication is always the transmission of a reawakening. And from this point of view the world is a process of progressive reawakening, thanks to which each soul manages to see itself from whatever point of view. The task of knowledge is not so much to reduce an experience to the 'I', as much as to build an equivalence between all 'I's. Knowing reawakens us in a consciousness that has been and remains that of others: knowing doesn't just mean corresponding with the self-consciousness of others, but also and above all observing oneself from another's point of view. This continual inversion of the position of subject and object constructs a subjective equivalence between 'I's. Translated into terms of experience, this means the universal equates to the translation of every experience into another's experience which occurs through the cycle of reawakenings. It's as though the bed from which we view the world were to grow slowly larger until it accommodated all things and all people.

Instead of hiding the bed away in secret and inaccessible rooms – and continuing to pretend that the nocturnal disintegration of the ego is incidental – we ought to learn to rethink and rebuild cities starting from these psychic switches. The city would then become a landscape for disappearance and reawakening rather than for action and labour. Work is leaving the city and establishing itself more and more at home: the only possible answer is to carry our beds into the streets. The city would then become a single infinite soul that is constantly disappearing, reawakening and changing skin each time it opens its eyes.

10

PETS

My mother always refused to allow dogs or cats in the house. The regular begging on knees from her three children could never shake her firm resolve. The only exceptions she would make were small animals that could be easily confined to small spaces: canaries, hamsters, fish, tortoises. None of these would pose any threat to domestic order (not that such a threat existed) but nor would it raise any doubt over the fact that this house was a human space: built by human beings and therefore suitable for anthropomorphic beings alone.

Homes, without us realizing it, have been transformed over time into machines created to separate our life from that of other species, to make free cohabitation mutually impossible. The adoption of some rare example of non-human life within domestic walls certainly does nothing to quell fears about biological diversity: the home remains the expression of our war against other species, or rather of all species against each other.

The reasons for this separation – the causes of this war – are mysterious. Homes, especially in the city, are monocultural plantations that actively fight against every form of biodiversity. The modern-day home first and foremost adopts an active genocide against everything that doesn't belong to our species. It's as though we're afraid that living creatures (apart from dogs, cats, canaries, parrots, blackbirds or mice that manage to cross our thresholds) might place our very identity in doubt.

In recent years, philosophy has regularly drawn attention to the choice which has led some people to fence themselves off in a sanitized domestic or urban area, and it has always attempted to define human life starting from its relationship of companionship – not biological, not purely material, but psychological and emotional – and coexistence with other species. Donna Haraway has written one of the most important manifestos of recent times on this question. And yet she is not insisting on companionship that can be ended by war. In the face of war, morality is not enough. The justice that ends war can be founded only on a new political order and not on simple, voluntary behavioural change by individuals. We need to reject the idea of difference, the notion that species are to be regarded as different from being to being, in just the same way that we fight against the idea of ethnic difference or class difference.

It was Plato who indirectly suggested this conclusion in one of his best-known myths. In *Protagoras* (320d–322c), Plato tells how the immortal gods wanted to create forms of mortal life, so they entrusted two giants, Prometheus and Epimetheus (literally, he who thinks about things first and he who thinks about them afterwards) with the task of giving appropriate powers to every species. Epimetheus asked if he could be in charge of the distribution, and to some species he gave 'power without speed', to others speed alone; to some, weapons of attack and defence, to others, the opportunity to hide because they were tiny or to save themselves because they were enormous. Epimetheus sought to balance out the distribution of skills to make it impossible for each species to become extinct. He gave furs, hooves and thick hides to those that had to withstand the cold. He then decided how these species would feed, the order in which each could eat the others, regulating in this way how easily they could reproduce. It was only when the range of faculties to be distributed had been used up that Epimetheus noticed he had forgotten one species, the human: 'all animal species were conveniently supplied with everything, whereas man was naked, barefoot and defenceless'.

It is hard to imagine a more dire prospect. Biodiversity is the result of decisions made by a foolish and inept divinity (Epimetheus could be translated as 'the incompetent') who unfairly divides the faculties that distinguish each species. Species are not defined according to what they are but what they have; it's a matter of wealth and property and not of quality and nature. To be a squirrel or an oak tree, a pheasant or a streptococcus, a mushroom or a parrot, is the result not of a battle for survival but of a process similar to that through which resources are divided between a group of individuals. The many ways in which life is expressed, then, does not constitute an ontology, but an economy of injustice: it's the sign of an arbitrary act, the result of a whim in the distribution of what by nature should belong to no one.

In this economy of diversity, humanity is the life form that remains outside the distribution – a non-species, the proletariat of living beings. For all species, identity is defined by the possession of a faculty. Humanity, on the other hand, has no property and no endowment. It's from this resentment that war arises. On the other hand, it provokes a sort of Bovaryism, the wish to be like other species.

Faced with the injustice caused by Epimetheus, the myth continues, Prometheus sought a remedy. From Hephaestus and Athena, he stole power and technology, which could be used to manipulate matter and reality, and gave these to humans. His solution allowed the initial imbalance to be rectified, but only through the creation of another inequality: the extra gift allowed humanity to ascend the hierarchy. The gesture that ought to have remedied the injustice produced another, more radical injustice. It's interesting to note in this story that technology is the attempted way out of the perverse game: clocks, computers, cars, wardrobes and houses are the tricks we have adopted so that we can pretend to be healthy, normal animals, in possession of everything we need to survive, like all the others. It is technology, moreover, that defines the existence of religion, the debt humanity pays for managing to overturn its condition of inferiority in relation to other living beings. In fact, according to the myth, it is only after the gift of fire and technology that the worship of the gods begins. Even language is a consequence of technology: it's like the callus on the effort the human species has had to make to repair its own inferiority in relation to other forms of life.

Yet technology, Plato continues, was not enough to defend humans from the cruelty of animals. People had to learn the wisdom that enables them to live together – 'politics' – to be able to defend themselves. And it was only then that the war against other living beings began, 'because the art of war is part of the art of politics'.

Politics and therefore the city provide the mythological setting for a new separation between living species: the revenge perpetrated by one species against all others, in reaction to a division of identity, wealth and powers, which it had recognized and perceived as unjust. Every city is the symbolic and material celebration of this reversal of order and multi-species hierarchy: a combat between the David of life-forms and all the others, thought of as a Goliath, allowed the victim to become supreme ruler.

Emergence from this war is possible only by remembering that all our identities originate from the imprudence and absent-mindedness of a minor, rather dim-witted, short-sighted divinity. We need to call into question not only the supposed superiority of human nature, but the very nature of all species – the very existence of what we call 'species'. The nature of any form of life is simply the expression of a wrong: every trait is something that could have belonged to any other species, and vice versa, any individual could or should have received another form. Just as in the case of ethnic or class identities, in biology we only have an identity because we lack something: all identities are the sign of a lack and not of something positive. A less consolatory argument has to be put forward in regard to the acquiescence shown by biology, politics, the various theologies, but above all by ecology, in the face of the supposed evidence of ontological separation of the species. Identity is the greatest injustice. The order that separates one species from the others, that defines the respective positions of the various living species in the network of life, is the political history of an injustice.

The new home ought therefore to be the place

for the destruction of every taxonomy, for the break-up of biodiversity (seen as a war between species). We ought to learn to build homes in which we no longer know if we are humans or canaries, cats or plants. The home of the future ought to be the space for a life that corresponds with the break-up of all species, a life which, to quote Karl Marx, has 'a universal character by its universal suffering and claims no particular right because no particular wrong but wrong in general is perpetrated against it'.

We gain a partial experience of this life, which is the complete loss of all identity, each time prolonged cohabitation with a household pet allows us access – beyond their anatomical or physiological difference – to a sort of basic emotional and cognitive 'humanity' shared by all species. When we succeed in building a relationship of intimacy – in other words, a domestic relationship – with one of any living form, the biological distance that separates us on a taxonomic level becomes purely incidental, like hair or eye colour. It's not enough to extend the number of species that live under one and the same roof: the home must become the space in which we can liberate any kind of life, without any further definition. Every loving relationship aims to liberate an anonymous life that belongs without distinction to both individuals who come together: everything belongs to everyone, and any claim becomes petty. This should happen when individuals belong to the same species as well as when they belong to separate species or realms.

11

FORESTS AND
GARDENS

After just a few days my language had changed. I no longer returned home: I went back to the forest. I didn't leave home: I came down from the forest. The change of language was the more superficial symptom of a deep psychic transformation. I kept repeating to myself, for example, that my love for skyscrapers came from the fact that they allowed me to rediscover the feeling that *Hominini* must have felt inside the ecological niche in which they had emerged: the branches of trees. I seemed to have realized that my body wasn't made for walking on the ground, but for spending days perched between one branch and another. It wasn't simply a mad impulse. The bedroom window went from floor to ceiling and what I could see were mostly the branches of trees that came up from the balcony of the floor below. Only through the leaves did I manage to glimpse the skyscrapers, which rose a few hundred metres in front of the bedroom, and the park beneath. Each morning, when I woke, I had the impression of opening my eyes in a human nest that had settled by chance in the canopy of an enormous tropical palm. The balcony that opened onto the living room was inhabited mainly by trees four metres tall. It was hard to say whether I was the joint tenant of a forest installed in the mineral structure of that tower or whether it was the trees that kept me company each day, as a dog or a cat might do. It was difficult to work out whether living in that apartment meant I was echoing the choice made by Cosimo Piovasco di Rondò – the central character in Italo Calvino's *The Baron in the Trees* – to live in trees, or whether instead it was the trees who had chosen to live there where humans lived.

The two towers of the Bosco Verticale (Vertical Forest), inaugurated in Milan in 2014, were designed by Stefano Boeri, who developed and radicalized ideas that had previously inspired Friedensreich Hundertwasser and Emilio Ambasz. They immediately became a global icon and were soon replicated in Holland, Egypt, China and Mexico. What struck me most during the few days spent within those walls was their capacity to transform the psychic experience of the city and the home. For centuries, cities have been built as a form of human mono-culture that associates individuals belonging to our species with blocks of stone: technically, they are projects for the desertification of the land. With this same gesture, the city has pushed to its margins all that has a non-human nature: this residential space has been called a 'forest', from the Latin *forestis silva*, the woodland found outside the city, or at its gates. Despite all the romantic passion generally associated with this word, *'foresta'* was originally the equivalent of 'a place for foreigners', a refugee camp for all those not formed like us. To think of forests as the solution to our problems, to think it's enough to increase the biodiversity of this refugee camp for non-humans – but not within urban monocultures – is equivalent to the attitude of those who, when they are faced with the phenom-enon of migration and raise the hopeless question about ethnic identity, argue that foreigners ought to be helped out 'in their own homes'.

In that apartment the opposites that have char-acterized modern architectural and urban culture became unthinkable. Trees were no longer outside the city: they were inside the home. Or rather, they seemed to be the home itself. The forest was no longer a distant, exotic reality: it was a domestic fact. Beginning with the eighteenth-century French architectural theorist and philosopher Marc-Antoine Laugier – the first person to imagine that the original house built by humans had been constructed by tying together the branches of a few trees – European modernity has never ceased imagining that it could return to living in the forests, that it could build a house in the forest. The symbol of this romantic return to nature was the 'hut'. From Thoreau until today, the hut has played this symbolic role: embodying the most elementary model of the artefact, a house that hides the fact it has been built, that conceals its own artificiality, to become a *trompe l'œil* of non-human naturalness, as though it were an *acheiropoieton* image of early Christianity. Rather than taking the house into the forest, the Vertical Forest has brought the forest into the home. Instead of regarding nature as what came before history and modernity, modernity, with its most iconic symbol – the tower, the skyscraper – brought nature to us. In this inversion, the idea of the forest also seems to assume another aspect: for if the forest is a skyscraper, then every forest is a part of technology, of engineering, which has nothing 'natural' about it.

Transforming the forest into a part of the home also means modifying the domestic experience from another point of view. As a direct result of the massive presence of trees, the balcony was populated by a fauna of insects and birds that I had never seen before in Milan. It was as if the opening of the home to a species different from our own had exploded the very idea of living space or ecosystem: I had opened my apartment to trees, and they had opened their homes to birds and insects. The presence of one species no longer banished the others; the establishment of one species allowed others to arrive and settle. The home became a means for multi-species coexistence; the home of one species was the body of another. Home was, then, also home for others, a space already occupied by other living beings.

It is no coincidence that such a revolution in the idea of domestic space should occur through a redefinition of our relationship with trees. The home hasn't always been associated with the city. Being at home wasn't synonymous with being in the city or of wanting to build a home: it was nomadic, able to travel, and often built with organic materials rather than stone. It was the garden that turned the home into something urban, stable, fixed to the ground, and therefore mineral.

When humanity decided to bind its destiny to a group of trees or perennial plants that grew in one place, homes stopped travelling and became fixed to the ground, just like plants. It could be said in a certain sense that all urban dwellings, as fixed and immovable places, are a form of vegetal Bovary-ism. Jules de Gaultier had identified in the attitude of Emma, the central character in Flaubert's *Madame Bovary*, the symptom of a tendency that has nothing individually pathological about it, but which defines the profoundest feature of human nature: 'the faculty imparted by man to imagine he is different from what he is'. Humanity is not one form among forms, one species among species: it is the form capable of pretending or believing itself to be all others. Each time we fix our home on firm ground, each time we think of the home under the guise of the city, we are pretending to be plants, we are imagining ourselves as trees. The city is a group of human individuals who dream of being a forest.

The idea that it was the garden, and then

agriculture, that imprisoned the home in the city was long cherished by anthropology. Its first paradigmatic formulation was that of the renowned archaeologist Vere Gordon Childe, who described for the first time the appearance of agriculture around the twelfth century BC in terms of a 'neolithic revolution': in his view 'the first revolution that transformed human economy gave man control over his own food supply'. 'Man', he wrote, 'began to plant, cultivate, and improve by selection edible grasses, roots, and trees. And he succeeded in taming and firmly attaching to his person certain species of animal in return for the fodder he was able to offer, the protection he could afford, and the forethought he could exercise.'[5] The 'urban revolution' is just a consequence of agriculture and of the possibility of accumulating and conserving food in the same place for a long time. The city is an emanation of the garden.

If this insight, restated more recently by French gardener and botanist Gilles Clément, is taken seriously, then it transforms the very idea of home. The homes we live in are really projects of multi-species origin: homes can only exist where there are trees or plants. And vice versa, domestic plants that we nurture in our living rooms bear no reference to what exists outside the city but are evidence of the fact that our home has stopped moving only because it is fixed to some form of vegetal existence. It is our love of plants that has allowed us to forgo our nomadic lives; it is the obsession with gardens that has allowed us to set up home in the city. Gardens are never the opposite of the urban fabric: they are its original nucleus.

If it's because of plants that we have entered the city, it is only thanks to them that we've managed to 'become civilized': it's because of them that we have lost our 'wild' nature. Forests are what prevent us from being savages. A 'savage' or 'wild' nature doesn't really exist, and never has done. Contemporary anthropology has freed us from the idea of the 'savage' in the human world, which is no more than the remnant of contempt and mindless racism that every self-conscious culture directs against the foreigner: the presumption of superiority is an optical illusion with which every culture views others. Every culture tends to regard 'the Other' as savage. 'When we make the mistake of thinking that the Savage is governed solely by organic or economic needs,' wrote Claude Lévi-Strauss in his masterpiece *The Savage Mind*, 'we forget that he levels the same reproach at us, and that to him his own desire for knowledge seems more balanced than ours.'[6]

We have learned to think that in no culture would there be a greater proximity to 'nature', just as no culture suffers for 'excess of mediation'. In the same way, cultural difference can never be interpreted as a moral preference: no culture can achieve Good more readily than another.

And yet, if the label 'savage', along with that of 'primitive', has been rigorously excluded from historical and scientific discussion relating to different human cultures, it is still very much present in discussion of the non-human. We still say that any space in which living beings build a world without the contribution of the human species is 'wild'; we make every effort to describe as human any form of life that comes close to its own Good and the conditions for achieving perfection.

'Wild' acquires a double meaning when it refers to non-human life, as William Cronon showed in his celebrated essay *Uncommon Ground: Rethinking the Human Place in Nature*, which launched an extremely important and wide-ranging debate in

1996. According to Cronon, the history of this notion and the paradoxes it generates are tied to religious and neocolonial prejudices. On the one hand, the idea of wild or savage (in the United States it is called 'wilderness') feeds on the myth of the frontier, which presupposes that the North American landscape was uninhabited, ignoring the massacres of local populations by the colonists. On the other hand, the desert, previously considered in negative terms as a satanic place in which all morality has ceased to exist, has undergone a kind of sublimation which has transformed it into a site of divine encounter and therefore into a place where moral improvement can be sought.

The myth of nature as wilderness, expressed in the idea of the natural park, is therefore a reversal of the founding myth of the modern state. Nature, there, is seen as that which preceded the state and civilization: the arrival of human beings sought to replace, correct and suspend the state of nature. In the myth of 'savage' nature, however, the city imagines an exteriority through which it can purge itself of the excesses of civilization and balance them. From this point of view, 'savage' or 'wild', when applied as an attribute to non-human beings, performs the opposite role to the one it has when applied to human cultures: it doesn't disparage, but rather exalts in that which is, supposedly, devoid of culture and technology.

Humanity is considered perhaps technically superior, but morally inferior to other species. By supposing non-human species lack reason (and therefore artifice and culture), it is believed that living beings in the 'savage' state are purer and more authentic than human beings: they cannot make wrong choices, because they are incapable of moving away from what is for their own Good. Due to their lack of subjectivity and freedom, non-human beings can never distance themselves from their own Good. While biology, thanks to Darwin, has helped us understand that human life is no different from that expressed in other forms, it continues all the same to conceive of non-human life as being governed by this absolute and unfailing adherence to its own nature and perfection. In this view, natural history is not morally contingent: evolutionary choices made mechanically through competition necessarily produce a local and global utility and promote the achievement of the 'best' for the species, and for the whole.

It's impossible to imagine that non-human life can make wrong choices. It's impossible to imagine there are errors, misunderstandings and catastrophes brought about by 'thoughtlessness' in non-human species. There is said to be a teleological order that allows all non-human lives automatically and unconsciously to attain Good and perfection. This logic of utility, implicit in every instance of evolution, represents, then, a form of rationality morally superior to human rationality. It allows non-human communities to exist without a historical context, without any trace of civilization, without accumulating and transmitting knowledge. It is this theological prejudice (it is scientifically impossible to demonstrate that non-human life tends alone towards its own Good and that evolution always makes choices beneficial for the species) that lies at the origin of all discussions of the 'savage' as an order morally better than the political order produced in humanity and the world of artifice.

To overcome this prejudice, to break free of the 'savage', it's not enough to say that man is an animal species: we need to fight against the tendency towards idealization that affects both human and non-human life. There is a perfect equivalence – not just cognitive but above all moral – between all species. All lives are morally ambiguous. None is endowed with natural ethical perfection. That's exactly why we all need to build homes, and no one is automatically at home on this planet.

On the other hand, what our relationship with plants seems to suggest is that we ought always to build our homes while connecting ourselves to other species. It's impossible to autonomously achieve our own Good and to perfect our own particular identity, because the fate of every species is in the hands of other species. All species make their own homes by building on the life of others. The whole planet is an immense suburb in which life never stops carrying out its own wonderful building speculations.

KITCHENS

For years I didn't know how to cook. It wasn't a partial ignorance – it was a radical alienation from the whole series of processes that allow certain portions of the world to become edible. I wasn't just ignorant about the way an onion had to be peeled and cut: I hadn't the faintest idea that onions were a regular ingredient in the dishes I ate each day. I had no idea what a sauce, a sauté or a stock was.

I wasn't the only one to blame. The education I was given had enormous gaps in everything to do with self-care and standing on my own feet, not just when it came to food. The fact that every human being needs to work and specifically to transform the matter and space around them in order to eat seemed a truth too complex and too esoteric to be revealed to a socially maladjusted adolescent like me.

These were the years of the great fashion for

industrial food: for a thousand reasons, dinner arrived at our home ready-prepared, ready-cooked in tins or coloured packs that required minimal handling. Food had always seemed a given, like a pebble, or a cloud, as spontaneously produced as the chocolates that Aunt Mimi assured me came from a mysterious chocolate tree hidden in one of the rooms of her house. No imagination was needed, no hand ever had to be lifted in order to cook. This blindness, entrenched in particular by my being a boy, was more an act of faith than a real experience: there were people around me who cooked, and above all there were people who cooked for me, and yet they remained invisible.

But the problem wasn't just moral or a question of awareness. Not knowing about cooking, not knowing how to cook, means, literally, not being in the world; it means being kept ignorant of the true relationship that ties us to everything that is part of the planet. The series of moves, practices, flavours and ideas that we file under the heading of 'cook-ing' are, in fact, not just the expression of our desire for physical or biological survival, and not a mere transient, incidental ornament for a few moments of our day. Cooking is both the reality and the symbol of our relationship with the world. We can be world, and become world, only by transforming it radically and letting ourselves be transformed by it. We can be world, and become world, only by constructing each time what Renaissance magic would call a 'sigil': a formula that enables and symbolizes the conjunction and transformation of a series of disparate elements.

Cooking doesn't just mean transforming what is around us: it also means establishing and preparing our own metamorphosis through what we cut or slice, grate or chop, stew or fry, boil or grill. It is the assembly of unrelated portions of the cosmos that no longer have the same aspect, the same form or the same experience. Each meal is a mutual initiation into a mystery in which the whole cosmos is summoned to participate. Onions, tomatoes, meat, grain, olives, but also our own bodies: the ingredients – literally those that enter the kitchen – will never leave in the same state in which they found themselves at the start.

Cooking is the transcendental form of every living being's relationship with the world and the planet for at least two reasons. First, the act of cooking demonstrates that our relationship with reality is not one of purity and absolute respect: we can have no intimate relationship with the world without transforming it. We are cooks of the world: we never stop cooking it, transforming it and transforming ourselves, and cooking ourselves together with what we cook. Everything is in a state of constant reciprocal manipulation. On the other hand, relating to the world never means being in front of it in the same way we might be at the front of a stage. There is no contemplation – or maybe contemplation is just one of the ways of cooking the world. Cooking is the evidence that there can be no autochthony: there is no immediate non-transformative connection with a space, a land, a place or a group of living beings. And above all, there is no pre-established order on which to rely. To carry on existing in the world we need to cook it: to sear it, to chop it, to leave it to thicken, to change its savour, taste, aroma and shape. We need to go 'against nature' – against its apparent nature and against our own apparent nature.

On the other hand, we can inhabit the world only by merging with it and letting ourselves be penetrated by everything around us. Cooking doesn't just involve the sacrifice of plants, mushrooms or animals, it is also about a sacrifice of the self: we will never be the same person after the meal, and that is why we need to eat. Likewise, to be at home, it's not enough to find ourselves in a physical place and give form to it: it's impossible to be at home without traversing the bodies of others and letting ourselves be traversed by the things around us.

From this point of view, all living bodies 'cook the world'; all living beings add tastes to the earth – not necessarily digestible and not necessarily pleasant. After all, as the distinguished interpreter of Indian thought, Charles Malamoud, has written, 'we should not contrast the world cooked [. . .] to some raw and natural world that might have preceded it. For in the final analysis, everything is already cooked such that all that remains is to re-cook it.'[7]

What cooks the world is none other than the fire contained in every living thing. Too often we forget that the energy that gives life to animals and plants is the solar energy that plants capture in their cells, that they breathe into the mineral flesh of the earth and supply to all living beings. An extraterrestrial component pulsates through our veins, and it is this same extraterrestrial energy that makes life possible. Every interaction with living beings is a form of cooking and transmission of light. Every experience is a way of cooking and allowing ourselves to be cooked by the world. Every living body is a world kitchen.

The strongest evidence of this strange configuration that binds together all living beings and transforms them not so much or not just into food, but above all into a kitchen of the self, is that extraordinary mammalian invention: milk. The bond between mother and child is the relationship of transformation of the self that allows the body of one to become accessible to the other and vice versa. Love is the kitchen of the self: nothing can relate to the other without transforming it and without being transformed.

Milk, however, is not the only instance of the wish to become food for others. In what we call 'fruit' or 'vegetables', plants experience the same metamorphosis that leads parts of their body to become a kitchen of the self and to bind themselves to individuals that belong to other realms (and do not differ by species) through a bond of mutual cooking. Through this prism we should also consider the dietary link that brings together a variety of species that we tend to view only through the metaphor of hunting. This image projects onto the world a sad illusion according to which what binds us to any other life is a form of inevitable predatory and sacrificial violence, so that the life of one co-incides with the death of the other. Every species is milk for the other species: there is never a pure encounter of one species with another species, because each body exists through the kitchen of the self. The identities of species are unstable realities: we always relate to others through the mediation of a reciprocal fermentation, in a vortex of metamorphosis that involves everything around us.

It is only in the kitchen that life can encounter itself; it is only by becoming milk that it can touch other forms. That is why nothing of what is alive is tied to a destiny. Every dish, every meal, is an invention of flavours, of colours, of textures that have nothing to do with the present moment. The world is a kitchen since, through living beings, it is constantly changing its own nature and its own form without the past being truly able to determine it. Cooking means always being able to produce a flavour, an aroma, a texture of the material that the given, the present, the immediate has never revealed nor seems able to produce. How could we ever

imagine the natural smell of wine or the smoky flavour of whisky from their ingredients? And how
far is it necessary to modify the world so that it can
produce that aroma that is obtained only in the
encounter between our body and others?

The kitchen is a form of divination capable of
projecting the world beyond itself. And in the end,
the domestic space in which such a rite takes place is
this: a crystal ball and an alembic that generate a
spiral of transformation in which raw or ready-prepared
species of vegetables and animals interpenetrate and
modify each other. From this point of view, the kitchen is the opposite of the garden: instead of a
juxtaposition of different species that live one beside
the other in a relationship of interdependence at a
distance, it produces a sort of implosion of space
and of identity, where everything must penetrate the
other and take on a quality that pertains to none of
the initial components.

The presence of kitchens turns our homes into
great ontological dressing rooms in which the most
varied forms of nature enter to reinvent themselves
as new cosmic characters. In the kitchen, every home
stops being a closed, proprietary human space. Pigs,
chickens, oxen, corn, cocoa, coffee, maize, hazelnuts,

pears, apples, bananas, lettuce: the most far-flung lives meet at this single point in the world to replace atom for atom the material of our body. It's in this space that we admit there is nothing human about us: like strange Frankenstein monsters we reincarnate ourselves in the life of lambs, pears, asparagus and porcini mushrooms. We take their flesh and we let them live through our body and our form: we are cosmic butcher shops in which dozens of different species die and return to life in other forms. And through kitchens, homes are transformed into enormous turbines in which everything enters the body of the other and everything changes appearance.

Having arrived very late in middle-class homes, the kitchen should really devour them entirely, become their new paradigm, transform them into a shared laboratory in which to change ourselves and the world so that we find each day – and each day in a different way – the right blend, the possibility of shared happiness. The new city ought to be a kind of crucible in which we seek the elixir of life by blending objects and ourselves, each one with the others, and with every type of object.

Philosophy ought to think about the city by starting from the home, and about the home by starting from the kitchen: that is what architecture is attempting to do thanks to the investigations of William Cronon and landscape architects Carolyn Steel and Dorothée Imbert. If urban space is considered from the viewpoint of the kitchen, we are forced to admit that cities are much vaster than we imagine: all non-human living beings that we generally exclude must form part of it. Human cities are impossible without wheat, maize or rice, without apple trees, without pigs, without cows, and without lambs. It's non-humans above all that make our cities habitable. And these same presences are what make our homes habitable. Everything that has no right to enter a kitchen enters it: it's a training ground for admixture, in which the dividing lines between things and people are suspended and the contrast between humans and non-humans is inverted into a joyous fusion.

There is also another aspect that makes kitchens embryonic examples of the way in which we should imagine and construct homes in the future. They are ambiguous and contradictory spaces: as domestic custodians of the fire through which each person can change the world, kitchens seem like ancestral remnants of a primitive humanity. On the other hand, the kitchen is the place in every house which is not only most heavily equipped with technical instruments, but becomes even a technological workshop, a factory, a place for invention, for artifice. The kitchen is the quintessential technical space, but it is above all the highest and most sublime form that technology can assume in our life. In the act of transforming the bodies of other living beings, as well as our own, in order to produce food, cookery demonstrates that real technique is always a form of care – an extreme and loving attention to ourselves and to others, a search for personal and shared happiness, the invention of a harmony that is both ephemeral and changeable, whose sole purpose is to allow life to lean towards pleasure and conviviality.

Conclusion

The New Home or the Philosopher's Stone

The era that has just started is different from all those – human and non-human – that history has recorded up to now. This is not the casual result of a slight deviation affecting a handful of elements on the landscape. Nor is it due to the appearance of new eyes and new minds observing the world.

The break with the past is much more important. It is not the people on the planet that have changed. It's the planet itself. Over the last decades, the Earth has experienced an unprecedented technological, biological, climatic and geological acceleration. A gigantic army of machines and artefacts has covered the world's surface, consuming enormous quantities of energy to keep itself going.

Thousands of species have vanished, trigger-ing unstoppable feedback loops that modify the ecological balance built up over centuries of shared evolution.

The new climate regime imposes variations on the life form and geographical distribution of plants and animals, irreparably shifting the balance of biomes.

Human activity has combined to transform the geological surface making it incomparable with the past.

We're on a planet different from the one known, described, painted and photographed by our ancestors.

It's as if we – people, plants, animals, funguses, bacteria, archaeology – have landed on another planet. No one has seen it before us. No one has seen its forms. No one has measured its force.

We are pioneers: new Eves and new Adams, compelled to explore the world, to give names to things, to burn our tongues on tastes that no one has ever tried, to graze our knees as we walk over territories uninhabited until now.

Yet, unlike the biblical myth, it is we who must transform this new planet into a garden. We have no way out. We have no other solutions.

We are not her daughters and her sons; the Earth

is not our mother. The connection is even stronger, more radical, more inevitable. We are flesh of her flesh. Our life is intimately bound to her body: we live in her body and on her body.

For we owe everything to stone.

We live primarily in stone buildings. They are no longer caves, but enormous mineral constructions that we shape into a whole variety of forms. We spend most of the day surrounded by stones of every kind. We eat, sleep, make love, cook, wash and revive ourselves in stone spaces. It's between stone walls of varying chemical composition that we think, imagine, dream, write, draw and create artworks.

Stones are not just the silent witnesses to our lives. They accompany us in other ways. We use stone and metal instruments to move about. We call them cars: glass and metal objects that feed on a strange form of liquid stone – petrol – and allow us to move about on the Earth. Other metallic objects, aeroplanes – also extracted from stone – allow us to move about in the sky. Still more man-made objects – boats – are made with a combination of metals and allow us to move about on water. Thanks to these modified stones, we can radically transform not just our own lives but that of the whole planet. It is thanks to them, indeed, that our species has not only radically multiplied its movements and redefined the flora and fauna of every space but has also modified geography itself. Stone is everywhere, even where there are seas and skies. And virtual stone corridors have opened to allow all species to change position, to migrate over the surface of the planet.

But above all, stone determines our lives today. It's in objects made of stones and minerals – computers – that all our memories and thoughts are recorded: in polymers, plastic, ceramic, copper, iron, nickel and silicon. Our brains are now made of the same substances as the planet. Our archives are made of the same material as the world. It is thanks to black stones – mobile telephones – that we can communicate with anyone over the whole surface of the globe. Through copper, silver, gold, tantalum, nickel, dysprosium, praseodymium, ter-bium, neodymium, gadolinium, silicon, oxygen, antimony, arsenic, phosphorus, gallium, and many others, the Earth allows us to connect with anyone. Our feelings now are transmitted not just through our own bodies but through the body of Gaia herself – through her stones. We never left the Stone Age, after all.

It's as if we were transferring more and more of our life into Gaia's body, turning the Earth into an appendage, a prosthesis of our anatomy. This epoch of the humanization of the Earth has been called the Anthropocene. We wanted to take over all the Earth's powers, take possession of the power of her stone, occupy her matter with our thoughts, our emotions, our lives. This was an unconscious form of narcissistic obsession: we demanded at all costs that our face be mirrored on the planet. We have sought to conceal its outward appearances.

We are at home everywhere: everything is or has been inhabited by humans; every portion of the globe has been transformed into a cosmic room, garage, kitchen, store cupboard or bathroom. One of the ways of describing the Anthropocene is that the planet itself has become home. There is no longer any form of externality; there is no longer any form of spatial alterity. The city is finished for the same reason: we can no longer leave home. It is not a question of quarantine or lockdown. The home has come to include so much world and so much 'planet' that no other space is left.

From the opposite viewpoint it can be said that home itself has become a planet. The planet has invaded us, its forces have entered us, its powers have shaped us. Being penetrated by Gaia means often having to change life, it means being compelled to transmit one's own life to other species, it means considering one's own form as a simple mobile configuration of life on the planet. That is also why the contrast between the local and the global, like that between internal and external, can be expressed only in terms of the contrast between terrestrial and extraterrestrial. But even when (or if) we escape to other planets, we'll have no option but to take our home with us – even if it is reduced to a simple spacesuit. We are condemned to replicate the domestic model everywhere.

It's difficult to gauge the consequences of this metamorphosis. First, it means the end of modernity, in terms of the illusion of creating and producing a substitute space for home. Modernity began by snatching production away from the domestic space, from the ancient *oikos*, and transforming the production of wealth into a public, political affair. The return of work to the home is just one of the first symptoms of the end of the modern period. It is now the planet-home that is snatching production from the cities, enabling it to become autonomous.

Cities had absorbed the life of the senses, channelling it into museums, department stores, panoramas and world fairs, and in doing so created the circus of shadows that has transformed life into an open-air carnival. This festive explosion of feelings has gradually wheedled its way into the home and has established itself there for good. Home is where, it seems, sensorial excitement has to happen. It is here that we make discoveries, meet others and see things like nowhere else.

In this new space, in this home that has become planetary in scale, it's as impossible not to be cosmopolitan as it is to claim a local identity: continents and nations are rooms in one single, vast apartment. Conquest is impossible: it would be like launching an imperial attack on the bathroom from the kitchen, or vice versa.

As the tragic heroes (Hamlet in particular) with whom modernity began have shown, it is impossible to establish a public space that is not assailed by a domestic truth that one would like to remove and erase. Especially when, even if everything is home, in this home everything remains unknown. At home there are now billions of people we know nothing about; at home there are forests and herds of animals about which we have not the slightest knowledge; at home there are objects about whose purpose and significance we know nothing.

Now that the home has become as large as the planet, any notion of geography and any notion of genealogy is demolished. Every tiny living creature is cooking the cosmos and preparing to change its flavour for ever. Every tiny portion of the planet has been cooked by fellow occupants of whom we have lost all trace.

The birth of the world-home marks the end of ecology too. Ecology was the first discipline to imagine the planet in terms of a single global domestic space. It was proposed in 1749 by Isaac Biberg, a pupil of Linnaeus, the Swedish botanist and taxonomist to whom we owe the system for the biological classification of living beings, in what is often regarded as the first major treatise on ecology (*Oeconomia naturae*). The reasons for this view were, at that time, theological. Most biologists, then, did not believe in the transformation or evolution of species: they thought all species remained just the same over the course of time. In such a context, the only way to know whether a relationship existed between a buffalo in Arizona and an Australian fly (and to understand it) was to adopt the viewpoint of the one who had imagined, designed and created both: God.

Since God was responsible for the existence of both, he must have devised and established a relationship between these two species, and between all living species. In Christianity, God relates to the world not as a simple governor or political leader relates to his people, but rather as a father relates to his family and to his home: he exercises power over the world only because he has created it. Likewise, the world's relationship to God is not like that of subjects to their sovereign, but like children to their father. The whole of life on Earth therefore constitutes a single home and a single family of the single Father-God. That is why Linnaeus and Biberg called this science the 'economy of nature'. The planet has been transformed today into the domestic space of one of its species – human beings – and this runs contrary to the perfect balance dreamt of by the great fathers of ecology. There is no longer any possibility of a 'natural' balance for the very reason that all living beings are at home (our home, the human home).

How do we live in a home that is as large as the whole planet? And in which ways might philosophy – always regarded as urban knowledge – help us? How can something different be done with the stones that have overtaken the Earth?

A long and ancient esoteric tradition has identified philosophy with chemistry. For centuries, it was called 'alchemy', the Arab transcription of a Greek word, *khemeia*, which means 'blend'. To think of philosophy as a form of chemistry means, on the one hand, rejecting any separation between thought and matter: thought is stone, a certain movement of stones. On the other hand, turning thought into a chemistry of the world, capable of transforming it into its own material structure, means imagining that every thought is an act of cosmic synthesis – which can reproduce that which exists or, in reverse, can just as easily introduce something new. Thinking no longer means representing and projecting an abstract form onto matter, but synthesizing a new one, and therefore materially changing the world. Every tiny material transformation is then itself an act of thinking, an idea.

It is through this new chemistry that we might save ourselves. This doesn't mean abandoning the age of stone or the home, but making stones and homes different, finer, more versatile. We have to try to imagine homes that can be transformed as rapidly as the weather. The task of alchemy was to synthesize the philosopher's stone: not to replicate another structure, but to locate the principle that makes it possible to transform any given stone into another form and therefore to assert the unity and equivalence of every centimetre of matter on the planet.

The home of the future ought to be this philosopher's stone: the principle that allows all things to transform each other, and each life to know it is equivalent to any other. If the home of the past was a machine that made distinctions, in the future it ought to become the collective discipline of blending: blending of classes, blending of identities, blending of populations, and blending of cultures. Homes will be the kitchens of the planet: inside them the Earth will find a new flavour.

Source Notes

1 Le Corbusier, *Le Modulor, essai sur une mesure harmonique à l'échelle humaine applicable universellement à l'Architecture et à la mécanique*, Boulogne: Éditions de l'Architecture d'Aujourd'hui, 1950 (translated from the French by Richard Dixon).

2 Ernst H. Gombrich, 'Style', in David L. Sills (ed.), *International Encyclopedia of the Social Sciences*, Vol. 15, New York: Macmillan/Free Press, 1968, pp. 352, 353.

3 Titus Livius (Livy), *The History of Rome*, Book 39, Chapter 41.4.

4 Baruch Spinoza, *Ethics*, Part III, Proposition 39 (translated from the Italian by Richard Dixon).

5 Vere Gordon Childe, *Man Makes Himself*, London: Watts & Co., 1936, pp. 74–5.

6 Claude Lévi-Strauss, *The Savage Mind* (1962), Oxford: Oxford University Press, 1996, p. 3.

7 Charles Malamoud, *Cooking the World: Ritual and Thought in Ancient India*, trans. David White, Delhi: Oxford University Press, 1996, p. 48.

Bibliography

Ábalos, Iñaki, *La buena vida: visita guiada a las casas de la modernidad*, Barcelona: Editorial Gustavo Gili, 2000

Aït-Touati, Frédérique, Alexandra Arènes, Axelle Grégoire, *Terra Forma. Manuel de cartographies potentielles*, Paris: Éditions B42, 2019

Allen, John S., *Home: How Habitat Made Us Human*, New York: Basic Books, 2015

Ambasz, Emilio (ed.), *Italy: The New Domestic Landscape*, New York: Museum of Modern Art, 1972

Attili, Giovanni, *Civita. Senza aggettivi e senza altre specificazioni*, Macerata, Italy: Quodlibet, 2021

Aureli, Pier Vittorio, Gabriele Mastrigli, Brett Steele, *Dogma: 11 Projects*, London: Architectural Association Publications, 2013

Bachelard, Gaston, *The Poetics of Space*, trans. Maria Jolas, London: Penguin, 2014

Banham, Reyner, 'A Home Is Not a House', in Joan Ockman (ed.), *Architecture Culture 1943–1968: A Documentary Anthology*, New York: Rizzoli, 1993, pp. 370–78

BIBLIOGRAPHY

Betsky, Aaron, *Making It Modern: The History of Modernism in Architecture and Design*, New York: Actar, 2016

Bilbao, Tatiana, *A House Is Not Just a House: Projects on Housing*, New York: Columbia Books on Architecture and the City, 2018

Boeri, Stefano, *Un bosco verticale. Libretto di istruzioni per il prototipo di una città foresta*, ed. Guido Musante and Azzurra Muzzonigro, with contributions from Michele Brunello, Laura Gatti, Julia Gocałek and Yibo Xu, Milan: Corraini Edizioni, 2015

Branzi, Andrea, *La Casa Calda. Esperienze del Nuovo Design Italiano*, Florence: Idea Books, 1984

Branzi, Andrea, $E = mc^2$: *The Project in the Age of Relativity*, ed. Elisa C. Cattaneo, New York: Actar, 2020

Brayer, Marie-Ange, Emmanuel Cyriaque, *Ant Farm Redux*, Orléans: Éditions-Hyx, 2007

Bryson, Bill, *At Home: A Short History of Private Life*, London: Doubleday, 2010

Celant, Germano (ed.), *Cucine & ultracorpi*, Milan: Electa Triennale, 2015

Colomina, Beatriz, *Privacy and Publicity: Modern Architecture as Mass Media*, Cambridge, MA, and London: MIT Press, 1994

Colomina, Beatriz, *Domesticity at War*, Cambridge, MA, and London: MIT Press, 2008

Colomina, Beatriz (ed.), *Sexuality & Space*, Princeton, NJ: Princeton Architectural Press, 2000

Colomina, Beatriz, Mark Wigley, *Are We Human? Notes on an Archaeology of Design*, Zürich: Lars Müller Publishers, 2016

Cronon, William, *Uncommon Ground: Rethinking the Human Place in Nature*, New York: W. W. Norton & Company, 1996

de Gaultier, Jules, *Le Bovarysme. La psychologie dans l'œuvre de Flaubert*, Paris: Librairie Leopold Cerf, 1892

de Kerckhove, Derrick, *The Skin of Culture: Investigating the New Electronic Reality*, London: Kogan Page, 1997

Elias, Norbert, *The Court Society*, Oxford: Basil Blackwell, 1983

Englert, Klaus, *Wie wir wohnen werden. Die Entwicklung der Wohnung und die Architektur von morgen*, Ditzingen: Reclam, 2019

Forino, Imma, *La cucina. Storia culturale di un luogo domestico*, Turin: Einaudi, 2019

Gombrich, Ernst H., 'Style', in *International Encyclopedia of the Social Sciences*, Vol. 15, New York: Macmillan/ Free Press, 1968

Gordon Childe, Vere, *Man Makes Himself*, London: Watts & Co., 1936

BIBLIOGRAPHY

Groys, Boris (ed.), *Russian Cosmism*, Cambridge, Mass. and London: MIT Press, 2018

Haraway, Donna J., *The Companion Species Manifesto: Dogs, People, and Significant Otherness*, Chicago: Prickly Paradigm Press, 2003

Harris, Marvin, *Cannibals and Kings: Origins of Cultures*, London: Vintage, 1991

Hayden, Dolores, *The Grand Domestic Revolution: A History of Feminist Designs for American Homes, Neighborhoods and Cities*, Cambridge, MA, and London: MIT Press, 1981

Heathcote, Edwin, *The Meaning of Home*, London: Frances Lincoln, 2012

Imbert, Dorothée, *Food and the City: Histories of Culture and Cultivation* (Dumbarton Oaks Colloquium on the History of Landscape Architecture), Cambridge, MA: Harvard University Press, 2015

Irace, Fulvio (ed.), *Storie d'interni. L'architettura dello spazio domestico moderno*, Rome: Carocci, 2015

Jaque, Andrés, *Superpowers of Scale*, New York: Columbia University Press, 2020

Kapp, Ernst, *Grundlinien einer Philosophie der Technik: Zur Entstehungsgeschichte der Kultur aus neuen Gesichtspunkten* (1877), ed. H. Maye and L. Scholz, Hamburg: Felix Meiner Verlag, 2015

Kegler, Karl R., Anna Minta, Niklas Naehrig (eds), *Raum-Kleider. Verbindngen zwischen Architekturraum, Körper und Kleid*, Bielefeld: Transcript Verlag, 2018

Koolhaas, Rem, *Elements of Architecture*, Cologne: Taschen, 2018

Lane, Barbara Miller (ed.), *Housing and Dwelling: Perspectives on Modern Domestic Architecture*, London and New York: Routledge, 2006

Le Corbusier, *Le Modulor, essai sur une mesure harmonique à l'échelle humaine applicable universellement à l'Architecture et à la mécanique*, Boulogne: Éditions de l'Architecture d'Aujourd'hui, 1950

Leonardi, Cesare, Franca Stagi, *L'architettura degli alberi*, Milan: Lazy Dog, 2018

Lévi-Strauss, Claude, *The Savage Mind* (1962), Oxford: Oxford University Press, 1996

Lovelock, James, *Gaia: A New Look at Life on Earth*, Oxford: Oxford University Press, 1979

Ludmer, Josefina, 'Literaturas postautónomas 2.01', in *Propuesta Educativa*, 32: 18 (2009), Vol. 2, pp. 41–5

MacIntyre, Alasdair, *After Virtue: A Study of Moral Theory*, Notre Dame, IN: University of Notre Dame Press, 1981

Mack, Arien (ed.), *Home: A Place in the World*, New York: New York University Press, 1993

Malamoud, Charles, *Cooking the World: Ritual and Thought in Ancient India*, trans. David White, Delhi: Oxford University Press, 1996

Marx, Karl, *Critique of Hegel's 'Philosophy of Right'* (1843), trans. Annette Jolin and Joseph O'Malley; ed. Joseph O'Malley, Cambridge: Cambridge University Press, 1970

Molinari, Luca, *Le case che siamo*, Milan: Nottetempo, 2016

Moore, Jerry D., *The Prehistory of Home*, Berkeley, CA: University of California Press, 2012

Morineau, Camille, Lucia Pesapane (eds), *Women House*, Paris: Manuella Éditions, 2017

Neutra, Richard, *Survival Through Design*, Oxford: Oxford University Press, 1954

Perec, Georges, *Species of Spaces and Other Pieces*, trans. John Sturrock, London: Penguin, 1997

Rybczynski, Witold, *Home: A Short History of an Idea*, London: Penguin, 1990

Rykwert, Joseph, *On Adam's House in Paradise*, Cambridge, MA, and London: MIT Press, 1981

Schiller, J. C. Friedrich von, *On the Aesthetic Education of Man: In a Series of Letters*, trans. Elizabeth M. Wilkinson and Leonard A. Willoughby, Oxford: Clarendon Press, 1967

Scott, James C., *Against the Grain: A Deep History of the Earliest States*, New Haven, CT: Yale University Press, 2017

Shorter, Edward, *The Making of the Modern Family*, New York: Basic Books, 1975

Simanowski, Roberto, *Facebook-Gesellschaft*, Berlin: Matthes & Seitz, 2016

Simmel, Georg, *The Philosophy of Money* (1900), trans. Tom Bottomore and David Frisby, London: Routledge, 1990

Sparke, Penny, *The Modern Interior*, London: Reaktion Books, 2008

Steel, Carolyn, *Hungry City: How Food Shapes Our Lives*, London: Chatto & Windus, 2008

Steel, Carolyn, *Sitopia: How Food Can Save the World*, London: Chatto & Windus, 2020

Taut, Bruno, *Ein Wohnhaus*, Stuttgart: Franckh'sche Verlagshandlung W. Keller & Co., 1927

Taylor, Charles, *Sources of the Self: The Making of the Modern Identity*, Cambridge: Cambridge University Press, 1989

Teyssot, Georges (ed.), *The Domestic Project: Man's Home – Archetypes and Prototypes*, Milan: Electa Triennale, 1986

Vidler, Anthony, *The Architectural Uncanny: Essays in the Modern Unhomely*, Cambridge, MA, and London: MIT Press, 1992

BIBLIOGRAPHY

Vidler, Anthony, *Warped Space: Art, Architecture, and Anxiety in Modern Culture*, Cambridge, MA, and London: MIT Press, 2001

Viollet-le-Duc, Eugène-Emmanuel, *Histoire d'une maison*, Paris: J. Hetzel, 1887

Acknowledgements

I started writing this book before, and without the least suspicion that, the whole of the planet was closed in their homes for months. This strange coincidence literally transformed a work about the house into a work about the world. But, above all, it made time stand still. The dates refer to the time of writing and not to the time of publication.

Many people have reviewed parts of this book and have helped me to improve it. Many of its pages have been nourished by discussion with others.

I wish to thank Giorgio Agamben, Frédérique Aït-Touati, Annalisa Ambrosio, Marcello Barison, Stefano Boeri, Arianna Brunori, Barbara Carnevali, Hervé Chandes, Michela Coccia, Emanuele Dattilo, Chris Dercon, Alessandro de Cesaris, Cecilia Granara, Donatien Grau, Fabian Ludueña, Laura Maeran, Annalisa Merelli, Annalisa Metta, Alberto Parisi, Philippe Parreno, Philippe Quesne, Camille

Richert, Paolo Roversi, Bas Smets, and Michele Spanò.

Finally, I'd like to thank Paolo Repetti for the generosity with which he welcomed me into his home, Rosella Postorino, who taught me to write, and Maria Luisa Putti, who introduced me to the sacred mysteries of the Italian language.

I dedicate this book to my daughter: for six years home has been everything that can be possibly done with and for her.